Anything Bu

Anything But a Quiet Life

Ideas of God in the Bible

•

Theodor Jaeckel

SCM PRESS LTD

Translated by John Bowden from the German
Wer sich stören lässt, lebt.
Die Entwicklung des Gottesverständnisses in der Bibel,
published 1988 by Quell Verlag, Stuttgart

© Quell Verlag 1988

Translation © John Bowden 1989

All rights reserved. No part of this publication may be
reproduced, stored in a retrieval system, or transmitted,
in any form or by any means, electronic, mechanical,
photocopying, recording or otherwise, without the prior
written permission of the publisher, SCM Press Ltd.

0 334 01874 9

First British edition 1989
published by SCM Press Ltd
26–30 Tottenham Road, London N1 4BZ

Phototypeset in Great Britain by Input Typesetting
and printed in Great Britain by
Richard Clay Ltd, Bungay

Contents

Preface ix

Part One: Belief in God in Biblical Times

I From the Exodus from Egypt to the Babylonian Captivity 3

  1. The beginnings under Moses: God's call out of slavery to freedom and responsibility 3
  2. The development of the cult: Yahweh or Baal? 6
  3. The prophetic criticism: election means obligation 8
    What are prophets? 8
    The prophetic aim: social cohesion 9
  4. The interplay of religion and politics: the worship of God as a guarantee of national greatness? 10
  5. The message of the prophets 13
    Amos: The righteous God judges 13
    Hosea: The merciful God endures 15
    Isaiah: The merciful judge calls for repentance 17
    Jeremiah: What may the believer expect in a disintegrating world? 20
    Ezekiel and the Second Isaiah: Trusting God in a strange land 21
      The God of the whole world 21
      The two ages 24
      The productive power of suffering 24

II From the Babylonian Captivity to the Beginning
of the Christian Era 26

   1. Judaism in a foreign land: The preservation of
national identity 26

   2. The Priestly Writing: A collection and survey of
the religious heritage 27

   3. Nehemiah and Ezra: Religion as a law for priests 29

   4. The books of Jonah and Ruth: Protest against the
narrowing of the religious aim 30

   5. Job: Life is for those who are willing to be
disturbed 31

   6. The apocryphal writings: belief in angels and in
Satan 32

   7. Daniel and the writings of late Judaism: trust in
God under the pressure of alien rule 34
      Joy in the law of God 34
      The comfort of the beyond as a goal of faith 35
      The 'revelations' of the 'last day' 38
      Messianic hopes 39

   8. 'When the time was fulfilled': The special position
of Judaism in the world of Mediterranean religion 41

III The Message of Jesus 43

   1. Jesus' understanding of God: A link with the
prophetic tradition 43

   2. Jesus' attitude to God's commandment:
An unconditional concern for men and women 45

   3. Jesus' attitude to the expectation of salvation:
The kingdom of God is possible today 46

   4. Jesus' consciousness of his mission: The authority
of the one sent by God 48

   5. The call for repentance: God reassures by
disturbing people 49

   6. The misunderstanding: 'We hoped that he would
redeem Israel' 50

   7. Jesus' basic concern: self-development in
partnership 51

IV	The Origin of Christian Faith	54

1. Easter and Pentecost: The discovery of a new
   way of life   54
   The appearances of the risen Christ: Light
      over the cross   55
   The significance of the Easter events: Renewal
      through the venture of trust   56
   Holy Spirit: The new awareness   57
   The religion of the cross: Suffering as a
      productive force   58

2. Paul   60
   His life   60
   The Damascus experience   61
   The end of the law   62
   Hope for the perfect world   63

3. The Gospels: A call to discipleship   67

4. Jews and Christians: The common task   68

Part Two: Belief in God Today

1. The discovery of God as a challenge to growth   73

2. A modern view of the biblical understanding
   of life   79
   The meaning of the biblical term 'God'   80
   The language of faith   82
   'Resurrection' and 'eternal life': Opening up
      a new sphere of life   83
   The kingdom of God: Social salvation or
      redemption of the soul?   86

Postscript   91

Dates in biblical history   93
Map of Palestine   97
References to the Bible   99

Preface

For much of my life I have worked in China and Japan, where my task was to explain the biblical understanding of God in colleges and in local churches. In doing so I discovered that the heirs of a serene culture going back over thousands of years were rather put off by the brash Western Christian way of talking about a personal God. Their philosophical and religious tradition is pantheistic. There is no way which leads from it to the God of the Bible. But as close observers of the world and human circumstances the people of Eastern Asia are realists. I found that I caught the attention of my audience if I could demonstrate in literature, art and history or even in the course of one's own life that in the biblical view a moral loss of face did not compel one to abandon the social group to which one belonged, whether through disappearing, committing suicide or cutting oneself off from it in some other way. That was in contrast to views in Eastern Asia. I was able to say that a request for forgiveness and the granting of forgiveness was socially possible for God's sake, i.e. because it had a religious foundation, and was useful because it allowed a new beginning. That led on to a conversation about the value and worth of life.

The pessimistic mood of a general anxiety about life offered a similar point of contact. People in East Asia thought with resignation: 'Because suffering constricts the possibilities of living I shall keep as inconspicuous and quiet as possible in order not to encounter it.' However, those in the biblical tradition can say confidently: 'Although I too have to go through dark and narrow places, I do not fear any misfortune because you, God, are with me to guide me.' This attitude made people prick up their ears. If the conversation worked, a bridge had been built to a biblical understanding of God which had been tested in practice.

In that way I learned to seek from the Bible not primarily what it said about 'God', but what it said about how men and women behaved and what they were seeking. This small book is the result. It describes in a popular way the development of the religious consciousness in the 1300 years of biblical history.

I have particularly enjoyed the work for two reasons. One cannot recognize from the beginning how the story to be told will end. The movement is not along a constantly ascending straight line; it proceeds in fits and starts, in surprising shifts; indeed, some of these have to be corrected later.

The result is not a product that can be taken away and consumed. It is grains of wheat which bring forth fruit depending on the ground in which they are put. The Bible does not promise either a healthy society in this world or a state of spiritual repose in the next, but points to the possibility of making use of the opportunities to become an instrument of the good and in so doing to gain courage, composure and knowledge. It calls us to go through the endangered world with this aim in view. The way is laborious but rewarding; it brings life to everyone, even the unprivileged, and makes it worth living. My account of the Old Testament period and my comments on Paul go back in the first place to a book by Guy Daniel, *The Bible Story*, London 1955. A list of the main references to the Bible appears at the end of the book.

Oberursel near Frankfurt   Theodor Jaeckel
March 1988

PART ONE

Belief in God in Biblical Times

I | From the Exodus from Egypt to the Babylonian Captivity

1. *The beginnings under Moses: God's call out of slavery to freedom and responsibility*

The history of Israelite religion does not begin as a gradual appearance of divergent themes but with the profile of the person of Moses. Under his leadership, around 1250 BCE a few thousand Hebrews broke out of slavery in the cultivated land of Egypt. They had led an ordered life there; their material needs had been taken care of ('the fleshpots of Egypt'), but they had to do what they were bidden. They freed themselves from this life of social and political dependence and took the shaping of their course through history into their own hands, first of all wandering as shepherds in the expanses of Arabia and later settling in the villages and towns of Palestine.

The first written accounts of the Exodus from Egypt were written down between three and four centuries later. We are not concerned here with the details of what really happened at the time of Moses but with the religious consequences which a subsequent period drew from it. What significance was attached to that power traditionally called 'God' in connection with the departure from Egypt and the start of a history for which those involved in it took responsibility themselves?

In antiquity religion served to justify the interests of tribes and states. As a result the ancient religions disappeared with the downfall of the communities on which they were founded. Not so the religion of Israel. Granted, as we shall see, from time to time Israelite religion, too, served to justify the ends of the state. But from the beginning the Israelites also understood their God as a critic of their desire to justify themselves, and therefore the religion of Israel survived the collapse of its state.

The biblical writings with their historical accounts, sagas, biographies, songs, collections of laws, letters, sermons, utopian visions of the future and scientific explanations span a millennium. Therefore as a whole they say more about 'God' than what was already said at the beginning of this period. But the bond which holds this literature together is made up of three convictions which go back to Moses. Even today they shape the culture which has been influenced by the biblical religion.

1. At that time it was customary for peoples to tell their deities what they expected from them – fertility and success in war. When they were disappointed in these expectations they looked for other deities. By contrast, Moses convinced the Israelites that they had not sought God out; rather, he had sought them out. God had led them out of Israel and delivered them at the Red Sea. They were his people, chosen to carry out his task.

That is reflected in the agreement which was made between God and the people of Israel on Sinai. Unlike other peoples, the Israelites did not make any conditions for God, but accepted God's conditions – the moral demands of the Ten Commandments. Later this task was extended to the call to be the messenger and witness of God for all peoples – 'a light for the nations'.

God had chosen Israel (Amos 3) to do more than just reproduce itself, even at the expense of others. Nowadays we would say that Israel was to hold firm to the meaning of life and manifest it. One might call this *shalom*: the ordered world and a flourishing life together in community. We might use Jesus' term 'kingdom of God' or Paul's 'being in Christ crucified', or the evangelist John's 'bringing forth fruit'; or we might call it love of God and love of neighbour. This gives human beings a goal and says that that goal is to be reached by venturesome trust.

2. The second commandment is: 'You shall not make any image or likeness of God, worship it or serve it'. Worship without imagery is Moses' second great achievement. On their wanderings and in their battles the Israelites took with them a tent as God's dwelling place. In it was a wooden chest, a religious shrine, the ark with the agreement between God and the people whom he had chosen. Other peoples had religious shrines for their images of God. However, there was no image of God in this shrine but God's word: two stone tablets from Sinai bearing God's commandments. Instead of a symbol of human wishes there was a communication from God to humankind. God made himself felt in the conscience.

The peoples of that time symbolized their conception of God with powerful, terrifying statues of rulers or with images of fertility. Even the Israelites did not live without having a conception of their God. However, this understanding of God was not a rigid one; it could develop in the course of time.

3. When Moses was feeding his father-in-law's sheep in the steppes east of Elath, he had a shattering religious experience. It is described as fire burning in a thornbush without consuming it, and as the voice of God which addressed him from this fire and called on him to free the Israelites from the slavery of Egypt. When Moses asked the name of the one who had given him this commission, so that he could refer to him when he spoke to the Israelites,

the answer he was given was 'I am present'. God's being and activity are all-embracing. Today he is with men and women, and he will also go with them tomorrow; he is interested in purposeful, responsible human action.

What the biblical religion – indeed what any religion – says about human responsibility is therefore a reliable interpretation of its image of God. If we are to have an understanding of the manifestation of the God of the Bible which does justice to reality we need also to investigate the particular aims in life which were followed in individual periods of the history of biblical religion.

2. *The development of the cult: Yahweh or Baal?*

On leaving Egypt the Hebrews had been confronted with Moses' understanding of God; but they did not continue to maintain this level. They were wandering groups of shepherds who camped in tents and lived by rearing goats and sheep. Their existence was insecure and wretched. Their survival depended on finding access to springs and either getting the better of rivals there or coming to arrangements with them. Therefore their numbers had to be as large as possible and their leadership as strict as possible. It was important to be wise, cunning, adventurous and if necessary even to secure the survival of the group by force. They had no experience of settled living as a culture. The individual identified himself with his community.

In the course of time they learned agriculture and settled. To obtain good harvests they needed fertile soil and favourable weather conditions. They warded off bad neighbours, repressing them or killing them. Waging war was a divinely-willed matter, necessary for reasons of safety.

The individual could not exist without his group. He did not stand over against the community, but felt himself above all to be a member of it. It was important for the group to have good leadership. The individual contributed to this through loyalty to his leaders. Behind the leaders stood the tribal god, who justified their existence and their decisions. If the leadership was competent and implemented the interests of the tribe, this god had proved himself and therefore had a claim to thanks and worship.

The Israelite did not have any individual experience of 'God'. For him religious experience was something that bound him to all the members of his tribe. (Even now we can get an impression of this from the common prayer of Moslems in public places.) 'God' did not encounter him in conscience and in personal prayer but as the destiny of the community into which he was born and which he had to accept. There was no individual piety with questions about the meaning of illness and death. The idea that God was concerned that human beings should be good had not yet made its mark.

The Israelites' understanding of God was like that of the peoples round about them. However, they called their tribal God Yahweh, while the gods of the other peoples each had a different name. But when Israel had settled and was concerned that its agriculture should be fertile there were disputes and indeed a vigorous struggle over the name of the God to be worshipped.

In their transition to the higher culture of an agricultural society the Israelites had learned that the forces of fertility were Baals, lords, who under this name – or even a proper name – were worshipped in well-laid-out groves and in 'high places'.

That raised the question whether the local Baal had now taken the place of Yahweh or whether Yahweh had taken the place of Baal. Or could one perhaps even allow a place to both side by side? All three possibilities were practised. For the basic question with which Baal or YHWH was approached, namely, 'How can our community survive?', was answered by both in the same way, with the demand for an appropriate cult to be performed regularly.

3. *The prophetic criticism: election means obligation*

The situation became markedly different only with the appearance of a new type of man of God: Amos, Hosea, Isaiah and their disciples. They re-established the old idea from the time of Moses that religion is not primarily to do with the cult but with morality. The aims of the nation were subordinated to the fulfilment of the task for which God had chosen his people.

What are prophets?

The forerunners of the prophets were men like Samuel and Nathan in the time of David, around 1000 BCE. Elijah was active a century later; it is reported of him that he experienced God not just as a shattering natural event but already as a word in the stillness of the heart.

'Prophets' were originally a phenomenon of Canaanite religion. They were groups of strange people who worked themselves up into an ecstasy by wild dancing, received the spirit and inspiration of their God and let this babble forth from them. Anyone who behaved like this was called a *nabi*. When the Israelites entered the country, they took over this behaviour, and groups of such *nabi*s formed in honour of Yahweh. Gradually, however, a purified concept emerged, so that the cruder forms of spirit possession disappeared. What was left, though, was the conviction that someone who was inspired could reveal the spirit and the will of God. As the one who proclaimed the will of God the seer was called a prophet.

He represents God and calls for repentance: Samuel calls on Saul to repent because he spared the spoils of war from destruction; Nathan calls on David to repent because he killed Bathsheba's husband Uriah; Elijah calls on Ahab to repent because of his illegal appropriation of Naboth's vineyard. We also come across divine possession or inspiration outside Israel in the case of the priestess of the Delphic oracle. She too calls for repentance, albeit in an enigmatic way; when Croesus of Lydia asks whether he will conquer Persia he is given the famous ambivalent answer: 'You will destroy a great kingdom.' The shamans, too, are possessed by God, but they do not call people to repentance. However, the Israelite *nabi* hears the will of God and hands it on openly. In this way he becomes the model of the true suppliants of the future, whose concern it is not to twist God's will to their own desires but on the contrary to open themselves to the will of God.

The prophetic aim: social cohesion

When the Israelites gave up their wandering existence they took possession of land and houses. In village and town they came to have neighbours, friends and enemies. Various professions developed. The political problem of how to get on with one another had to be rethought.

The Egyptian culture which they had left behind them had been a hierarchical one. Those below obeyed those above. Those above were nearer to the heavenly order and had the task of commanding 'those below' and at the same time supplying their needs. The Israelites did not like this political structure. Therefore they gave themselves an order in which all members of society were equally distant from heaven – or equally near to it. Of course they had different rights and duties in this framework. But in contrast to the conduct of other peoples, theirs had to be socially responsible. Dependence was not to degenerate into oppression and exploitation even in the case of aliens who came to them. For God had liberated them all together from the 'slavery' of the Egyptian form of society.

After the settlement it had no longer proved possible to maintain this social order. The structure of possessions had changed. Prosperity and power came together. Money was lent out at exorbitant rates of interest. If a debtor was unable to pay, his land was confiscated. The courts supported the powerful. The independent smallholder disappeared; he sank to becoming a leaseholder, a serf or a slave. The great landowners built splendid town houses for themselves. (The difference between poor and rich was like that in France before 1789 or that in Russia before 1917.) The official religion did nothing for the oppressed. It was concerned with the well-to-do who appeared punctiliously at worship and who offered the requisite sacrifices.

Amos, Hosea and Isaiah savaged this attitude. They said that the oppression of the poor and the ritualistic worship of God which was practised by holding orgies was faithlessness towards God. Without a social conscience the community was rotten and would not be able to offer any resistance to invading enemies. The land was not the property of those who possessed it; it belonged to all because it was God's property. Therefore it had to be administered for the good of all.

Amos and Isaiah showed up worship and cultic celebration, along with its hymns, as being false reassurance unless it had social commitment. Since their time religious people have felt restless if they are not involved in remedying social injustice. Movements like the co-operative societies go back to the convictions of these men.

4. *The interplay of religion and politics: the worship of God as a guarantee of national greatness?*

The worship of Yahweh kept the Israelite tribes from being swallowed up by their Canaanite environment. It also welded the individual tribes together so that they could offer common defence in their conflict with the coastal power of the Philistine cities (the Phoenicians). That happened under tribal leaders who were called 'judges'.

It then proved that they had to stand together not only in

times of war but also in peace. With the anointing of Saul as king a central state power was established. With Jerusalem David gave the state a capital in which he concentrated the worship of Yahweh and so strengthened the central power of the state. From that time on state power and religion were organized centrally and related to each other.

In 926 BCE the northern tribes broke away from the south in opposition to Solomon's son. Now there were two Hebrew states, which occasionally even waged war against each other; however, they felt linked by their worship of the same God. The northern state called itself 'Israel' (the southern state called itself 'Judah') and disappeared after two hundred years as a historical entity. It succumbed to the Assyrians in 721 BCE.

An important factor in the composition of the Old Testament proved to be that at that time refugees from the northern state brought to Jerusalem old legends and historical accounts from the early period of Israel which had been written down only shortly beforehand. A written version of these narratives had already been prepared in Jerusalem around a century earlier. As it was thought undesirable to have two divergent accounts, a team worked on producing a combination of them. The result of this effort occupies a substantial part of Genesis and Exodus.

As the redactors fortunately did not smooth out all the unevennesses, historians can get behind them to what are presumably the original versions. The northern version is called the 'Elohist' because in it God is called Elohim; the rather earlier southern version is called the 'Yahwist' because it speaks of God as Yahweh. It is to these redactors that we also owe early collections of material in the books of Amos and Hosea,

The prophets saw to it that Israelite worship of God did not remain a religious glorification of national greatness which would have gone under with the downfall of the state. Thanks to the prophets, the God who revealed himself in Israel from the time of Moses on became a power which offered to all who felt themselves addressed by this God a pointer through life which could be used even under adverse circumstances.

The prophets had disciples who sought to influence public life in the same way as their masters. They had little success; the state side did not fall into line. So they summed up their programme of social and cultic reform in a memorandum and set this down in a quiet corner of the neglected temple in Jerusalem for posterity. Decades later this work was discovered during repair works and read aloud to the then king, Josiah. He was so moved by its content that he elevated it to become the basic law of the state. It was called Deuteronomy – Second Law. Its instructions are put in the mouth of Moses as the law of God handed down on Sinai. There God and his people make their covenant. So we find the Ten Commandments both in Exodus (ch.20) and in Deuteronomy (ch.5). In addition to the two versions by the Yahwist and the Elohist, which recount the early history of Israel, we thus have as a third variant the Deuteronomic version, which seeks to infiltrate or to suppress the earlier narratives. A further version came into being during the exile in Babylon; we shall be concerned with it later.

Under King Josiah, the inhabitants of Jerusalem were optimistic about the capital, Jerusalem. They thought that they had found a way back to the true God of the time of Moses and therefore that they had his support in the national interest. The nation had a good conscience about God. They could assert themselves and even expand between the great empires of Assyria and Egypt, which were paralysed by inner difficulties.

Then in 609 BCE something incomprehensible happened. Josiah was killed at Megiddo fighting against Egypt; and soon afterwards, in 597 and again in 587, Jerusalem was conquered by the Babylonians, who had replaced Assyria as the world power. The prophets Jeremiah, Ezekiel and the so-called Second Isaiah investigated the significance of this misfortune for their understanding of God. We shall be looking at their answers later. First, however, something more about their predecessors Amos, Hosea and Isaiah.

5. *The message of the prophets*

Amos: The righteous God judges

By around 750 BCE humankind had tamed fire, invented tools, built houses, was using machines, had developed an urban civilization and had organized state life. Human beings satisfied their desire for knowledge about their own existence by attaching themselves to mythical deities. They bowed down to them and countered the pressures of nature and society with religious rituals. Critical thinking or questions of individual morality hardly affected them.

Then in the next three centuries a new spirit arose which blew from the Mediterranean to the Pacific. Amos, Hosea and Isaiah in Palestine, Zarathustra in Persia, Gautama Buddha in India, and Lao Tse and Confucius in China were men with an understanding of God and the world which surpassed anything hitherto.

Israel produced the first of these men, Amos. He was not a philosopher or a wisdom teacher but a shepherd. He put forward the unaccustomed, exciting view that the external fulfilment of religious rites had no value in God's eyes; what God wanted was righteousness among human beings in the same way as righteousness prevailed between God and humankind.

Amos was aroused to anger by superficial religious practices in the midst of social abuse. He could not keep silent about them. He began his attack skilfully by taking up the nationalistic religious ideas of his time and then showing them to be inadequate, indeed to be a threat to existence, in the light of his new understanding of God and humankind. At that time people expected a day on which the national God would reveal his power, destroy the enemies of Israel and make Israel lord over them. This hope for the 'Day of the Lord' continually arose in the political longing of the Hebrews. It reached its climax at the time of Jesus. In the time of Amos the Israelites imagined a day of vengeance on their enemies. So Amos proclaimed in the market place to a crowd of people that God would punish the neighbouring kingdoms because of their misdeeds. He mentioned these misdeeds one by one. 'Ammon slit up pregnant women in Gilead in order to expand its territory.' 'Tyre did not think of the brotherly alliance but sold whole places – not just prisoners of war – as slaves.' 'Edom persecuted his brother people with the sword.' The hearers will have applauded every accusation, as for example we did when the Soviets were criticized for their invasion of Afghanistan. But then terror struck them. For Amos now mentioned Israel's transgressions by name: the oppression of the poor by the rich; junketing at the expense of the lower class; depriving the weak of their rights; church services with solemn music, choirs and collections instead of social justice! He ended threateningly with the assertion that therefore Israel too would be punished, and punished worse than the others. 'For the day of the Lord is darkness and not light.' Indeed they were God's chosen people, but this privilege did not allow any lax attitude, but put responsibility on them to act rightly. If they did not prove worthy of their election, external enemies, like the Assyrians, would annihilate them. Their rotten community would not be able to offer resistance. Only if they served God by observing justice and righteousness instead of trying to soothe him by ritual would he support them. Only in this way could the longed-for 'day of the Lord' bring salvation instead of annihilation.

It is not easy to grasp the enormous progress which Amos

brought. For centuries his understanding of God as a just God who also expects men and women to act justly has been part of our basic convictions. But Amos was the first to make it clear that if human beings experience injustice, God sees this as unjust, too. A century before Amos, Elijah had recognized that God speaks in our hearts with a gentle voice. Amos extended this insight to the claim that God's voice includes all the desire for righteousness which stirs within us. The conscience that reacts in a sensitive way comes to be a decisive value: a concern which our culture owes to the prophet Amos. Since him, men and women have experienced the holy God as the power which, in the unconditional moral law, can free them from the fetters which entrap them and make it possible to find new breathing space. By taking responsibility for the weak they discover themselves as autonomous selves.

Hosea: The merciful God endures

Amos thought that God was just and strict, particularly towards his own people. Privilege meant obligation. Soon after him Hosea had personal experience of God's mercy.

Destiny had it that, though he was a member of the educated class, Hosea fell in love with a prostitute – perhaps a temple girl. He was convinced that he could improve her, and married her. But she kept lapsing into her old way of life, though she would then return to Hosea. And so it went on. Hosea felt tied to this woman. If she lapsed, he suffered; when she came back and knocked, he opened the door. Though full of abhorrence at her action, he loved her so much that he could not turn her out of the house. His whole hope was that she might finally return and stay with him.

Hosea was seized by God's holiness as much as by his passion for this woman. He detested the superstitious practices which went on in the cultic places; they had corrupted his wife and burdened his days. Like Amos, he too was clear that God's judgment had to break in on his faithless people like a storm. However, Hosea thought that he could not have abandoned his faithless wife because he loved her. Could God love less than human beings? Amos had made it clear that what human beings felt to be wrong, God must also feel to be wrong. If he, Hosea, could now continue to love his wife despite all her failings, could it not be true that God, too, loved his elect people despite everything? So Hosea found that the just and strict God was also a merciful one.

In Hosea 11 God tells how he freed the children of Israel from slavery, but how when they arrived in Canaan they turned to the Baals, so that he decided to put them under Assyrian rule. However, while he is thinking about all this, God sighs, 'How could I give you up, Israel? How could I surrender you? My heart is moved; my mercy is too passionate; I shall not give vent to my hot anger. I will not contradict myself in such a way that I destroy you; for I am God and not a human being, a holy one in your midst, and do not come to destroy.' Hosea could not say how these two sides of God were to be reconciled; on the basis of his own experience he simply knew that righteousness without mercy was not righteousness. He wanted to establish that.

'I am God and not a human being.' Down to the time of Amos and Hosea men and women formed their gods in their own image: lusting for power and pleasure, unpredictable, prone to vengeance and jealousy. Since Amos and Hosea this image of God has disappeared. God now appears as one who is just and holy, merciful and wise.

Today it is sometimes claimed that when we talk about God we merely project an ideal conception of ourselves on to heaven. The Bible sees things differently. Amos says: 'The Lord reveals his secret to his servants the prophets.' The authors of the biblical writings are convinced that God has revealed himself to them. The revelation of God's judgment is not welcome comfort which supports human expectations but a knife which lays open the thoughts of the heart and discloses damage to soul and spirit.

Isaiah: The merciful judge calls for repentance

Isaiah was a younger contemporary of Hosea. He lived in Jerusalem and moved in court circles. As the king's confidential adviser he guided him in matters of foreign policy.

Judah and the hill stronghold of Jerusalem lay between the rival empires of Egypt and Assyria; however, the main route did not go through Jerusalem but passed it by along the coast. If Judah restrained itself it could hope to remain untouched by the dispute between the great powers. So Isaiah advised the king that his strength lay in keeping quiet and trusting confidently. This recommendation showed a good sense of the political realities; but Isaiah interpreted the course of the world in principally religious terms by asserting somewhat naively that God guided history, moved people and nations to do his will and attain his goals. That people in general and the Israelites in particular often acted contrary to the will of God and brought his plan to nothing did not fit with this assertion. But Isaiah could cope with that, since he thought that he could detect a remnant of those faithful to God who accepted the assertion that God moves human beings and directs their history. So he gave one of his sons the symbolic name 'A-remnant-returns'.

This idea of the 'remnant of those who return' also solved the question which Hosea had left behind. Hosea had set alongside Amos's understanding of God as a condemning judge his own belief in God's mercy; however, he had not succeeded in associating the two ideas. Isaiah achieved this by recognizing that God was interested not only in the people as a whole but also in part of the whole – a new manifestation of God's purpose for humankind.

Isaiah also thought that God had to punish his elect people

for their wickedness, but that a 'remnant of those who returned', trusting God and obeying him, would survive the punitive judgment imposed by the Assyrians and form the nucleus of a new holy and righteous people.

Isaiah's conception of the remnant of those who returned, who trusted God, gives the individual his or her significance in religion. Hitherto in religious terms the individual had been a subordinate part of the community. Hosea had counted on God's mercy, but the future of the people seemed gloomy to him, because like all Hebrews before Isaiah he thought that God had made his agreement with the people as a whole and therefore had to punish all of them – guilty and innocent alike – for the wickedness of the majority. Isaiah saw things differently. He expected that God would send Assyria as the rod of his anger to punish the sins of Judah, but would save those who turned to him. And he foresaw a time in which those who returned would do God's will, ground the people's existence in righteousness and live in a state of prosperity, *shalom*. They would dwell in Jerusalem under an ideal king, a descendant of David. He embodied salvation; his name was wonderful counsellor, eternal father, prince of peace.

Here for the first time in the expectation of Israel there appears the conception of a perfect king. Later he was called God's anointed, the Messiah. The Christian church understood – as many people still do today – this and similar hopeful expectations as prophecies of Christ. Historically that is incorrect, for Isaiah speaks of the ideal king as one who has already been born, though his existence is hidden.

We may note three of Isaiah's insights:

1. In his view, God does not punish or reward the people as a whole, but carries the minority of those who turn to him and bear witness to him before the world into a new political community under an ideal king in righteousness and peace. Isaiah's notion of a remnant of the people of God which 'returns' and is therefore saved is a step towards the indivi-

dualization of religion. This course was followed further from Jeremiah and Ezekiel to Jesus, and the argument as to whether God's kingdom – righteousness and peace – takes shape with the help of the pressures of state or in the obedience of a religious confessing community which is ready to suffer has gone on in Jewish history since that time. Jesus, too, found himself confronted with this problem. Even on the day of the Ascension his disciples are said to have asked him, 'Lord, will you soon restore the kingdom to Israel?' What he understood by the kingdom of God, and what Paul and John the Evangelist understood by it on the basis of the experience of cross and resurrection, which was different from the expectation of the disciples, we shall see in due course.

2. By giving his son the name 'a remnant shall return', Isaiah pointed to return ('repentance') as a healthy influence on life despite any mistakes that are made. He shows God as a loving educator who neither spares those who go wrong the consequences of their actions nor rejects them. The offer of return gives people the possibility of painful and healthy growth. God was discovered as the merciful judge.

3. 'Unless you believe, you will not stand' (7.9). 'The one who believes does not flee' (28.16). 'Thus says the Holy One of Israel; if you return and be still you will be helped; in stillness and hope will be your strength' (30.15). With his commendation of confident trust Isaiah was the first to describe the nature of faith as the Bible develops it, using a number of figures as examples: from Abraham, Isaac and Jacob to Jesus and Paul (cf. Hebrews 11; 12). In the Bible belief is not an opinion with a religious colouring about something that cannot be proved, like some church dogmas, but is an attitude – the attitude of confident trust with which the mature person meets the demands made by destiny.

Jeremiah: What may the believer expect in a disintegrating world?

Like Isaiah, Jeremiah was active for more than forty years. He experienced the political downfall and cultural destruction of his land to the bitter end. The pious King Josiah had brought about a social and religious reorganization of the land in accordance with prophetic notions. But he fell at Megiddo. In 597 BCE Jerusalem surrendered to the Babylonians under Nebuchadnezzar. The intellectuals and those involved in making weapons were deported to Babylon. Those who remained once again relied on help from Egypt; Jerusalem was besieged again. The terrible conditions in the besieged city (including cannibalism) are described in Chapters 2 and 4 of the book of Lamentations. The city fell, was plundered and was largely destroyed. A further deportation of the population to Babylon followed. Only poor village-dwellers were allowed to remain, Jeremiah among them. Some 'patriots' killed the governor who had been appointed by Babylon, and then fled to Egypt. They took Jeremiah with them against his will. In Egypt he had to watch his fellow-countrymen turning from their God to the Egyptian goddess Astarte. We know nothing of Jeremiah's fate.

This man was a real *nabi*, one seized by God against his own wishes. Like his predecessors he had proclaimed the destruction of his people for their political, social and cultic misdeeds. He had to suffer for that. People, even his own family, turned from him. The police several times attempted to silence him. He was flogged, put in the stocks and exposed to the mockery of passers-by, imprisoned several times and during the siege of Jerusalem put in a muddy hole without food: a foreign slave saved him from death.

Jeremiah did not have a robust temperament. He did not like fighting. As the son of a village priest he would have liked to have worked a farm, had a family and lived an inconspicuous life. However, this was not granted him. His

God forced him to engage in public controversy so that he cried out, 'Cursed be the day on which I was born.' Jeremiah was not a religious hero but rather a man with a sensitive, questioning soul. His conversation with God was not the receipt of a command to which he acceded unquestioningly; nor was it an intercession for his people. It was a search for an explanation of his incomprehensible experience. In prayer he reflected on the God who had foredestined his fate and who made him an innocent sufferer.

Here he found the courage to go on. He came to see that his fellow-countrymen who had been deported to Babylon would spend a long time there. So he wrote to them (ch.29) saying that they should buy plots of land, build houses and start families. They were even to pray for the well-being of the state there, since their own prosperity also depended on that. He warned against an exaggerated religious patriotism, according to which God would soon have to make a return to 'his' city possible.

Does resignation perhaps underlie such a pragmatic attitude? That could have been the case, had Jeremiah lost his bearings. But he found a new orientation. He expected that God would enter into a new covenant with his people and put his law in their heart (Ch.31). In the midst of the misery of political and cultural collapse Jeremiah does not look back, but sees a clear sky ahead. Life is worth it, he thinks, even in such a hostile environment, if you use it to reflect again on your relationship with God – and thus also with yourself – and act accordingly.

Ezekiel and the Second Isaiah: Trusting God in a strange land

The God of the whole world

The end of the state of Judah with its national and religious centre Jerusalem, and the deportation of its leading classes to Babylon, put the Jews (as the Israelites are called after that period) in a difficult position. They suffered loss of political independence; homesickness, hope for return, resignation; they were tempted towards assimilation out of opportunism or through marriage. They were proud of their character as a nation and a religion in the midst of strange customs, which also exerted power; and they were members of a minority which was often mocked and at best tolerated. All this posed unaccustomed questions and called for decisions both from the community and from individuals in their everyday life. The answers were divided and sometimes contradictory. They were worked out in the two centuries between the capitulation of Jerusalem in 597 BCE and the reconstitution of the body of the people as a religious community with a temple of its own in Jerusalem by Ezra in 398 BCE. We find documentation for this period in particular in Ezekiel, in chapters 40-55 and 56-66 of the Book of Isaiah, in Haggai, Zechariah 1-8 and Malachi; in the so-called Priestly Writing, which has been incorporated into the first four books of the Pentateuch and the end of the fifth; and in the books of Nehemiah and Ezra.

Ezekiel, the son of a Jerusalem priestly family, was active in Babylon between 593 and 571 BCE. Another significant figure experienced the conquest of Babylon by the Persian Cyrus in 538. We do not know his name; because his sayings have been attached to the concluding chapter 39 of the original book of Isaiah as chapters 40-55 he has been called the Second Isaiah. What did these two prophets of the exile have to say to their companions in suffering? They could not continue the reproofs of their predecessors, since their message had to keep the Jews from despair. Otherwise there was a danger that they would turn from their God. So what did these two men proclaim?

To give encouragement to the individual, Ezekiel took up the insight of Jeremiah that 'everyone is punishable only for his own misdeeds'. The people understood the present national distress as the punishment for the guilt of former generations. Instead of this, Ezekiel taught that anyone who had sinned had already been punished with disaster or death. Thus his guilt had been expiated. Anyone who had remained alive had manifestly not sinned and could begin again unburdened. In the future everyone would be responsible only for his own actions or misdeeds. 'The soul that sins shall die; but if the disobedient person turns from his sins and acts justly, he shall live.'

Despite the former destruction of the whole people, individuals could now shape their future creatively. Free from the burden of guilt-feelings, they can feel that their actions are meaningful. For them God's presence could be experienced anywhere. It was possible to serve him even in a foreign land.

This message of hope was endorsed by the Second Isaiah, who provided a theoretical basis to the monotheism that was practised. He saw God at work even in the pagan ruler; he called Cyrus, who allowed the Jews to go home to Jerualem if they wanted to, the Messiah, the Lord's anointed! (Ch.45).

By being without a state, those in exile learned that God may not be tied to national interests but must be a God of the whole world. At that time the Israelites threw off the nationalistic husk of their belief in God. According to the teaching of the Second Isaiah, all the events from the creation of the world to eternity were connected with the one God. This new view associates the primal history of humankind with the history of Israel, and the history of Israel with the final future of the world. If God is at work in all this, people may approach the future with confidence. God has created the world, humankind and Israel and determined its existence hitherto; he will also do so in the dawning of the end-time.

The two ages

The Second Isaiah divides history into the time of suffering, which is now coming to an end, and the end-time of salvation, which is dawning. Israel stands at the centre of what is happening in both these times. Amos, Hosea and Isaiah did not have this division of the course of history into a period with tension and a period without. According to them, Israel and the other peoples were to be spared punishment for their misdeeds by turning to God; that called for a constant struggle for social justice. The earlier prophets did not know any succession of two ages, but spoke of the either-or of repentance as the decisive question which remains the same throughout the course of human history.

The Second Isaiah's prophecy of the end-time changes the moral command of the either-or into a temporal sequence of divine action. Decision on the future no longer lies with human beings but with God as the Lord of time. The Second Isaiah proclaims that the sufferings of the exile will be followed by a new time, free from toil: union with God, God's righteousness, salvation and grace, Israel's redemption, the faithfulness of the people to the law, peace and rejoicing – all this will last for ever; sorrow and sighing will flee. People may expect to be freed from the needs of life. According to Second Isaiah one may expect from God an existence without tension. This aim sets against despair of the harsh and confusing world the hope for an omnipotent God of the whole world who will create what we have not managed to. Whether such an expectation helps men and women to discover God's power or become mature remains to be seen.

The productive power of suffering

The Second Isaiah has another aim in his songs of the suffering messenger of God: the interpretation of innocent suffering as the possibility of establishing community.

Jeremiah was preoccupied with unmerited suffering, and

this was later also to disturb the author of the book of Job. Ezekiel developed the idea expressed by Jeremiah, that individuals are responsible before God only for their own actions, into a doctrine which said that those who experience suffering are not being punished for the transgressions of former generations but for their own. But in that case, why did some people who had not sinned suffer? The answer of the book of Job is that such suffering tests human fidelity to God. Second Isaiah announces that a good person can react creatively to unmerited suffering; it leads him to serve his neighbour. God says of his suffering messenger: 'Because his soul has laboured, he will see that it was not in vain. He will rejoice and have fullness of life. Through his knowledge he, the just, will make many just, for he bears their sins.' The eyes of the sinners are opened; in terror they recognize that the messenger of God has accepted suffering to the point of death so that they may be shaken out of their rut. They exclaim, 'He was wounded for our misdeeds and smitten for our sins; punishment lies on him that we might have peace, and through his wounds we are healed. We were all going astray, and each one looked to his own way, but the Lord cast all our sins on him.'

The innocent suffering of the messenger of God does not spare people from changing their views. Its effect is not reassuring but renewing. It is a productive force; it corrects those who go astray; it leads to conversion; it makes sick souls healthy and helps towards a mutual furthering of community life.

Doubt about the justification of unmerited suffering is resolved in these songs with the positive view that unmerited suffering arouses compassionate responsibility and encourages a strength which heals hearts and lives. The Bible uses the word love for it. By that it means concern. The one who suffers feels the pain; however, he does not just stand there lamenting, but adopts a constructive attitude of service.

II | From the Babylonian Captivity to the Beginning of the Christian Era

1. Judaism in a foreign land: The preservation of national identity

For the Second Isaiah, the God of the whole world called the Jews to be his suffering messenger among the nations. If they accepted what they had suffered so far, he would justify them before all the world and lead them back to Jerusalem. There they would win over the other nations to God as a result of their example.

The Jews agreed with the prophet when he said that their God was the God of the whole world. 'He measures the waters in the hollow of his hand and holds the heaven in his grasp; he contains the dust of the earth in a bushel; he weighs the mountains with a weight and the hills with scales.' But they found it difficult to represent this God all over the world, and to do so through suffering. Their nationalistic consciousness prevented them from accepting the Persian Cyrus as God's anointed. This title was reserved for a national king. Similarly, their sense of themselves militated against the prophetic understanding of the Jewish people as a suffering servant for other people.

The Second Isaiah asked the Jews: is your God to be a God just for you or a God for all people? Did the member of another people have to become a Jew in order to worship the creator and governor of the whole world, or would the Jews open the temple doors wide and make it possible for all who wanted to come in to find access to the God of the whole world?

When Cyrus allowed those who had been deported to return home, the Jews realized that most of them no longer wanted to do so. Jerusalem in a state of utter destruction was unattractive to people who had a comfortable home and a prosperous business. Only a few of them set out on the long journey, which was not without its dangers. That did not mean that those who remained in Babylon did not have any sense of a national mission. Quite the contrary.

Ezekiel and the Second Isaiah revitalized the old faith of God's chosen people. The Jews who did not return to Jerusalem had therefore to distinguish themselves as clearly as possible from their surroundings as a sign of their election. Mixed marriages were tabu; the old religious festivals were deliberately fostered; circumcision was elevated to be the sign of the true Jew. Because temple worship was no longer possible in Babylon, there was an emphasis on the sabbath: it was dedicated to rest, worship and reflection on the duties of God's chosen people. This gave rise to the synagogue service, the weekly gathering of the community for the praise of God, with prayer and reading from the holy scriptures.

2. *The Priestly Writing: A collection and survey of the religious heritage*

At the time of their deportation to Babylon the Jews had taken with them scrolls of scripture which contained their national legends, laws and history. These were worked over and summarized during the exile. The Pentateuch and the book of Joshua achieved roughly their present form at that time. On looking through the annals of the kings the redactors found reports of Baal worship at altars outside

Jerusalem and even in the temple there. They censured these in a stereotyped way. The various kings did either 'what was pleasing to the Lord', or 'what was not pleasing to the Lord', depending on the attitude of the individual rulers to these cults.

The editors summed up the ritual of worship and the rules for social conduct in one lawbook. In it they added new laws to those which had been handed down, like prescriptions for circumcision, the sabbath, synagogue worship and the many regulations for setting the Jews apart from their everyday environment. The redactors were priests, scholars, who by their work, which is now known as the Priestly Writing, sought to create order in the thought and life of the people. For example, they put a new account of creation in front of the old traditional account in Gen.2, in which God first modelled man from clay and then set him in the garden of Eden, finally making a woman as a helpmeet from his rib and bringing her to him. In this new story (Gen.1), plants and animals were created before men and women. It is worth noting that the redactors have handed down both accounts to us. They lead us to reflect on the gradual manifestation of God in Holy Scripture. The Bible is not the Word of God, but contains it. We must look for the Word of God in the Bible and can discover it there.

To give the Priestly Writing authority, its ordinances (mainly to be found in Leviticus) were embedded in the old history of the people in which Yahweh had handed down his law to Moses on Sinai. The first five books of the present Bible were called Torah – the instructions (of God). The Torah is a religious and ethical catechism presented against the background of the history of the people; there were readings from it in sabbath worship. There was no secular, political history-book alongside this book of faith, this history of faith. It therefore made a deep impression on those who heard it and continued to mould them.

3. Nehemiah and Ezra: Religion as a law for priests

The Jews from Babylon had several times begun to resettle Jerusalem with Persian permission; even a simple temple building had been consecrated. In the years after 444 BCE Nehemiah, with a patriotic group from Babylon, had attempted to do something about the wretched state of the Palestinian Jews, who had mixed freely with foreigners and threatened to lapse into national and religious indifference. But nothing important was to happen in Jerusalem until 398 BCE, when the priest Ezra appeared at the head of a large group. They brought with them the book of faith and the law which had proved to be the means of the people's survival abroad. It stressed the holiness of the elect people. By that the Jews meant reverence for Yahweh, and the need to part company with those of other beliefs. The way into a spiritual ghetto was the price for preserving their identity as a people.

Ezra was a man with a sense of mission. He was a scribe and had devoted his life to the study and implementation of the law. He was dismayed when he saw that the sabbath was not observed everywhere, that synagogue worship and the reading of the law was not carried on in an orderly way, and that many Jews had non-Jewish wives. A stop had to be put to that. He brought together and organized all those who felt as he did.

It was important to put all the social and religious life of the small Jewish community in Palestine in order. The convictions of Ezra's people proved attractive. A full assembly of the people was summoned. Ezra read aloud from the law, and the priests who had come with him from Babylon explained the significance of the new rules. The people gave solemn assent to a new agreement with God. From now on the law which had been read aloud in public was to apply. To demonstrate their conversion, men who had non-Jewish wives were to separate from them and marry Jewish wives.

Two hundred years earlier, at the beginning of the exile, Jeremiah had seen a day coming on which the remnant would return from Babylon with the knowledge of God written in their hearts. The length of the exile had put an end to these hopes. A remnant returned; however, their law was not written in their hearts but in a book that laid down in detail what God expected of his people. The people of a land had become the people of a book. The people had been constituted as a religious community, as a church. Therefore a Jew could continue to be a pious Jew even in a strange land: the book which directed his life went with him. But the understanding of the nature of serving God was narrowed: cultic rites had achieved the same status as moral commandments.

Prophets of the old kind could no longer be heard. They were no longer necessary. 'Thus says the Lord' had become 'Thus says the law'. When people wanted to know God and his will, they turned to his book. If they found an answer there, it was valid; if not, a competent interpreter had to be approached. The scribe had taken the place of the prophet.

4. *The books of Jonah and Ruth: Protest against the narrowing of the religious aim*

Not everyone agreed with Ezra's narrow understanding of fidelity to the law and the separation of the elect people. There were also people who followed the view of the Second Isaiah that the Jews were to bear the light of the knowledge of the one God into the world.

One of these was the author of the Book of Jonah. Jonah is the Jewish people who had been swallowed up by the Babylonian whale and were now cast up on their own shore in Palestine. Jonah's annoyance at the sparing of Nineveh from punishment expresses the way in which the law of God had been used to exclude other peoples from participating in the religious heritage of the Jews. The book is a protest against Ezra's aims.

The same is true of the book of Ruth. It sought to show that even King David counted a foreign woman – Ruth – among his ancestors. In this way it is polemic against Ezra, who compelled men who had married non-Jewish wives to put them aside.

Thus the great aim of the Second Isaiah remained alive. It says something for the religious maturity of the Jews that they accepted both these books, which were critical of official domestic policy, into the collection of their holy scriptures.

5. *Job: Life is for those who are willing to be disturbed*

The book of Job is also the result of the shattering experiences of the post-exilic period. It is part of world literature and discusses in dramatic form the question whether in view of the enigmatic character of our life there is a goal from which we can gain a meaning not only on solemn occasions but also in everyday life.

Job is the respected head of a large family. He can also look back on a successful life. Unexpectedly, however, everything begins to go downhill for him – in business, health and family, so that his wife turns from him and leaves him to himself. Then his friends think of him, visit him, and try to analyse his wretchedness for him. They seek its deeper causes and think that it is his basic religious attitude which is wrong, and that he must practise self-criticism. But the old man proves stubborn, and will not spit on his honour! There is a lively exchange of opinions, polemic, polarization. Both sides stop listening to each other: each party sticks to its position. No solution of the problem is evident. The atmosphere is tense.

Then something unexpected happens. The old campaigner who is sticking to his guns – objectively he was right

– understands that if he is set on his arguments he will lose his friends. On its last pages the narrative describes like this the spiritual change he undergoes, the way in which he becomes more relaxed, his new relationship with his friends and the fruits of the flexibility which he has regained: 'How shall I answer? I will put my hand on my mouth. I confess that I have spoken unwisely, said what is too high for me and what I do not understand. I give up this self-centred attitude and ask you, God, to teach me the meaning of my fate.'

Job is beginning to take a positive attitude to what fate has inflicted on him. He respects the experience of his limitations as God's guidance. He sees that if he persists in his arguments, however apt, he will not gain any real life, any community with others, but remain alone and ineffective.

His soul can breathe again. He no longer speaks against his friends but for them. 'God looked on him and turned his captivity, when he had prayed for his friends.' In this way a new, fruitful relationship develops; he has recognized God's guidance, which has frustrated and limited his life, as something that makes life worth living.

6. *The apocryphal writings: belief in angels and in Satan*

In addition to the recognized holy scriptures the Jews also had scriptures which were not recognized. Scribes might read them; otherwise they were banned from use in public and were regarded as 'hidden' – as we would say nowadays, their use was restricted. The Greek word for hidden is *apokryphos*, hence the term 'the Apocrypha'.

Their exclusion from public use did not last long, but long enough to deprive them of the same authority as the others. The attitude of the churches to the Apocrypha has varied. They were accepted by Luther as being 'not on the same level as the holy Scriptures (in their teaching authority), but useful and good to read (as a help to right conduct)'.

Like the Old Testament, the Apocrypha contains very different kinds of literature. The books of the Maccabees are historical accounts. The Wisdom of Solomon and Jesus Sirach are handbooks of moral and religious instruction. The Book of Tobit is a novel which was very popular at that time. It paints an attractive picture of Jewish family life. The son undertakes a dangerous journey to help his father and survives it without harm, protected by his companion, whom he does not recognize to be an angel.

Belief in angels had already developed powerfully in the two centuries before the composition of the apocryphal books. It was thought that God visited people and spoke with them. But the stronger the stress on God's exaltation, the less fitting such familiarity seemed. Therefore people switched to his messengers (in Greek *angeloi*, our word angel). Under Persian influence the number of messengers at God's disposal grew considerably. Their leaders, the archangels, were given names like Raphael, Michael, Gabriel. Finally everyone had their own guardian angel who represented them before God.

Angels could also be messengers of the evil one; in that case they were under the command of Satan. In former times the Hebrews had thought that it was God who sent both good and evil to humankind. In II Samuel 24 we are told how God moved David to do wrong and punished him for it. Persian belief in the two rival powers of light and darkness probably gave rise to belief in Satan. Satan is God's adversary. He appears in the Bible for the first time at the beginning of the book of Job; there he plays the role of a public accuser, commissioned by God to test human faith. From this there developed the idea of the devil, the deceiver, the adversary, who is at war with God. This belief was strengthened by the growing feeling that God cannot tempt human beings to evil. Thus the author of I Chronicles 21.1, written around 300 BCE, replaces the word God with the word Satan in the scene in which, according to II Samuel 24.1, God had led David astray to do evil.

How did it come about that other figures could enter into the relationship between human beings and their God? Was God's call to them to be responsible before him felt to be too pressing? Was too much confidence put in human capability? Had people learned to appreciate the realities of life better? In order to stand before God did they have to hold on to other heavenly powers and exploit them? The acceptance of angels, Satan and the devil into Jewish religious conceptuality shows that the Jewish aim in life was no longer clear. It had to be redefined. Would the final result lead into an impasse or to wider horizons, to spiritual impoverishment or to maturity?

7. *Daniel and the writings of late Judaism: trust in God under the pressure of alien rule*

Joy in the law of God

Ezra's reforms had made the temple the centre of Jewish life. At festivals the pilgrimages to Jerusalem were climaxes of religious and national life. For the rest of the year people had the synagogue service and the observance of the Torah.

The Torah regulated the course of worship. It prescribed the penalties for murder, manslaughter, drunkenness and the like. It contained rules for everyday life, for example as to what animals might be eaten, the periods of quarantine for infectious illness, medical clearance after healing, the observance of the sabbath rest, dealing with foreign workers, and so on. It covered life down to the smallest detail and was interpeted and developed by legal experts, the scribes, for any new situation which might emerge.

A code of conduct can mislead people into being more concerned with its precise observance than with the purpose that it is meant to serve. The Jewish 'law' also succumbed to this fate. But for Jews it was more than just a code of conduct; it was a divine institution, given by God directly to Moses on Sinai – the voice of God himself; so it was a cause for joy for every honest person.

People who felt this way were called Hasidim; we would call them 'pious'. Sabbath by sabbath they went to worship, and as it began they heard the time-honoured confession of faith: 'Hear, O Israel, the Lord our God is one Lord, and you shall love the Lord your God with all your heart, with all your soul and all your strength.' Then they prayed together and listened to the reading from the law and the prophets. They promised to love their God by observing the law. Here some people may have been thinking of some divine reward. But the ideal of a Hasid was to serve God by fulfilling the law, simply because this was right. Their poets, above all the author of Ps.119, praise God and his law in words which even now bear witness to the power and depth of their feelings.

The comfort of the beyond as a goal of faith

The law and the reverence shown to it had the effect of preventing the Jews from being assimilated during the exile in Babylon. Later, in Palestine, they came under Hellenistic Syrian rule, and their fidelity to the law was increasingly put to the test by the life-style of easy tolerance. This pressure led to two religious innovations: to belief in the resurrection of the dead and to the transformation of the old hope of an ideal political community into the utopia of a rule of God who would make a new heaven and a new earth.

When the pressure of Hellenistic culture also took political and military forms and in 167 BCE the Syrian king Antiochus Epiphanes transformed the Jerusalem temple into a shrine for Zeus, armed rebellion broke out under the leadership of the Maccabee family. The people admired the rebels, but two questions prevented many people from joining them. Had a small country like Judah any prospect of success in the face of a superior foreign power? And what was the reward for those who perished for the sake of the faith without achieving political success? A work which went from hand to hand in secret, the book of Daniel, answered these questions.

The book tells of Daniel, a legendary hero from the days of the Babylonian exile. After a summary of the four hundred years of Jewish history following the exile it gives a description of the terrors of the present. The book achieved its purpose. The discovery that one of its great men had been informed by God of all that was to happen gave powerful support to the Jews. So God had not abandoned them completely. And at the end of the book they were given real spiritual refreshment: 'Such a turbulent time will come as has never been from the beginnings to this day. At the same time your people will be saved, all who are written in the book of life. And many who lie sleeping under the earth will awaken, some to eternal life and others to eternal shame and disgrace.'

The prospect of the resurrection from the dead made possible a new answer to the problem of the suffering of the pious. The Hasidim who preferred to suffer rather than betray their God would one day be rewarded, but their adversaries would be punished. This view spread amazingly quickly, and produced a bewildering abundance of every possible view of life after death.

The rebels were joined by people who had been enthused by the book of Daniel and were able substantially to consolidate their position under Judas Maccabaeus. With the death of Antiochus the pressure ceased. His successor granted the Jews freedom of religion. The temple was solemnly purified and restored to its true purpose. Orthodox Jews even now celebrate this day of the year with a feast. But the Maccabees had tasted power. Now they called not only for religious but also for political freedom. They broke the peace treaty and fought for political independence. The parties of the Sadducees and Pharisees came into being at this time.

The Sadducees derive their name from a high priest of the time of Solomon. They were the party of the aristocrats and supported the high priest. They were ready to fight; but if fighting was senseless, they came to terms with the occupying power on condition that they retained their official position. The Pharisees were nearer to the people: they had emerged from the movement of the Hasidim. Their main concern was religious freedom. Whereas the Sadducees were prepared, if need be, to secure political advantage at the cost of religion, the ideal of the Pharisees was to keep religion pure, even if as a result they went into the political wilderness. That is why they were called 'Pharisees', 'separated ones'. After the death of Antiochus they had received the religious freedom they desired; why should they go on fighting for political freedom? This difference in political aims also led the two parties to have different world views. The ideologically conservative Sadducees rejected the new idea of a resurrection; they regarded such an innovation as a transitory spiritual fashion. That made the Pharisees attack them all the more zealously.

The controversy over political independence continued and in fact led to a separate Jewish state. The high priests made themselves Jewish kings; this again offended the Pharisees, who regarded anyone who was not a direct descendant of David as a usurper. The kingdom existed for sixty-five years as a free state. Then the Romans appeared in Palestine, and in 63 BCE Pompey captured Jerusalem after a siege of three months. Again the Jews were allowed no more than freedom to practise their religion.

The 'revelations' of the 'last day'

The Pharisees refused to support the efforts towards an independent kingdom; these did not match their ideas. On the sabbath those who went to worship heard not only the reading from the Torah but also that from the books of the prophets. They heard how the prophets expected the actual establishment of an ideal kingdom, in which justice would prevail under a blameless king. The book of Daniel with its promise of imminent redemption also made them hopeful. But these hopes collapsed when it became clear how the hunger for power was corrupting the Maccabaean leaders. They became men who put their political power above observing the law. The Pharisees were deeply disappointed, and therefore looked upon the arrival of the Romans with a certain grim satisfaction; however, at the same time they recognized that any hope of a state of Israel had to be buried for the foreseeable future. So they began to say that only God had the power to establish the kingdom. They could not imagine that he would not exercise his power; the time had finally to come in which Yahweh appeared on the historical scene to drive away all evil and establish his kingdom. Otherwise all the suffering of the Jews would have been meaningless.

The pressure of this hope produced new kinds of prophets. There could no longer be prophets who made known the will of God. The will of God had been made known; it was the observance of the law. Anyone who now attempted to preach anything that could not already be read in the law would not have been listened to. However, sensitive believers could not be happy with that and looked for a way out. They found it in the book of Daniel. They could not appear themselves, but people would listen to them if they attributed their message to some former great man. The result was a new form of literature, the 'Revelations' (in Greek Apocalypse). In them revered great men of the past looked forward to a splendid future. These apocalypses were composed between 200 BCE and 100 CE. The Bible contains three examples of them: the book of Daniel, the Revelation of John at the end of the New Testament and the summary of such a 'revelation' in Mark 13.

All the 'revelations' have certain things in common. The authors describe the visions of the future under the name of a hero of faith – Daniel, John, Moses. They all reveal that the 'last days' of the world have come and that the last chapter of history, determined by evil and the saving intervention of God has begun. The hope of the old prophets for a Jewish state under a descendant of David as a good king is transformed by the new visions into the expectation of an anointed emissary of God who will redeem the Israelites and rule the world. The author of the book of Daniel describes this dream of the future in almost ecstatic terms. The redeemer receives his commission from 'the ancient of days' (God): 'I saw in this night vision, and behold one came on the clouds of heaven like a son of man to the ancient of days and was brought before him. He gave him rule and honour and empire, that all nations, people and tongues should serve him. His rule is eternal, it does not perish, and his kingdom has no end.'

Messianic hopes

When the legions of Rome marched into the Jews' small land, the Jews had to resign themselves again to a lengthy period of occupation. When, they asked in despair, would they ever be free again? For people in such a mood the 'revelations' opened up a view into another new world. They promised people a new earth when God's kingdom came. With growing excitement people read that God had not abandoned his people; he was only waiting until 'the last days' had been fulfilled; then he would send his anointed to judge the nations and to avenge all the suffering of his people in the past and the present. The eyes of many Jews will have gleamed at the prospect of such a final reckoning with their enemies.

Only a very few of the apocalyptic writers maintained the hope of the Second Isaiah for a messenger who would rule meekly and at the same time be 'a light to lighten the Gentiles'. In Zechariah, amidst the cries of triumph about the imminent annihilation of the enemies of Israel, there is a gentle remark to Jerusalem: 'Look, your king is coming to you, a just man and a helper, poor, and riding on an ass.' The man in the street understood the coming of the anointed to mean that the heavens would suddenly open and that the anointed would triumphantly appear on the clouds amidst thunder and lighting. Some believed that the saviour would be born in secret – in Bethlehem, because this was David's birthplace; or in Jerusalem, because David had ruled there – and remain hidden until the time of his revelation before the world had come. Be this as it may, the result would be a day of judgment; and Jewish rule would replace the rule of Rome.

The relationship of people to God had essentially changed since the time before the exile. Amos had proclaimed, 'Seek good and not evil, and you will live.' God's command to do good still had validity; but what about the conclusion, that this would lead to life? Real life was unsatisfactory. Were the commandments of God too much of a demand on men and women? Or should a satisfactory life not depend on human striving for the good, but on God's activity? Was a satisfactory life perhaps impossible in earthly circumstances; did not circumstances need to be changed, in a way which could not be achieved by human beings but only by God? Did not obedience towards God perhaps have to be supplemented by hope for his intervention – with the danger of new disappointment?

The right way to the goal of life had become uncertain. Even the goal itself was no longer sure. Had the initial idea of a personal holy God who called human beings to responsibility been wrong? Perhaps good and evil were part of human life as it is destined to be. So the book called Ecclesiastes says: 'I saw all that is done under the sun, and behold all is vanity and a striving after wind. Love and hate, dispute and peace, all has its time. No matter how hard people work they have no gain from it. They cannot achieve the work that God does, either the beginning or the end.' What happens is attributed to God's activity; but no goal can be recognized. All that is left is the advice actively to enjoy to the full the portion of life that one is given: 'Eat your bread with joy and drink your wine with good cheer. Enjoy life with the woman whom you love as long as you have the vain life that God has given you under the sun. For that is your share in life and in your work.' The theme of our sceptics (like Jean-Paul Sartre) was already being discussed around 200 BCE – existentialism in the old Bible!

At a time of such ferment in Palestine a boy called Jesus – God helps – was born in the house of a craftsman. How would he answer the question of the right aim in life?

8. 'When the time was fulfilled': The special position of Judaism in the world of Mediterranean religion

At the time of Jesus, life in Palestine was no bourgeois idyll. In patriarchal social structures with serfdom and slavery the strong sought to make their way at the expense of the weak and the weak attempted to survive. The independent national state was a thing of the past and had been replaced by the rule of an alien imperial power. But it had not yet been forgotten, and a group of patriotic underground fighters, the Zealots, hoped to restore it.

In the Mediterranean world the religions largely played the role of some of our present-day national churches. All kinds of comfort for the future, in terms of this world or the next, were offered and seized, as real life was full of distress.

In this religious environment Judaism occupied a special position. With its Torah, the instructions of the creator God, and its Hasidim and Pharisees, it was a unique religious phenomenon. The search for individual happiness together with the social struggle centred on this instruction; responsibility for it absorbed the human will.

This was the cultural air which Jesus breathed. The modern world is very different. There may still be class struggles, but our social structure has incorporated new features; one can protest against it without being arrested. On the other hand, the whole social concern is no longer focussed on God's instruction. God is not the centre of modern thought, feeling and will. This different kind of cultural background must be noted if we are not to misunderstand Jesus' message of the 'Father in heaven'. This message freed people of Jesus' time from the pressure of the excessive legalistic demands of the Torah. In so far as our contemporary society takes note of Jesus' message about the Father, it tends to use it to free itself from the seriousness of the divine demand as such. Jesus saw the 'Father' as the one who lovingly teaches and guides his children; our modern sensitive contemporaries see him as a kind relative who intervenes in emergencies.

III | The Message of Jesus

1. Jesus' understanding of God: A link with the prophetic tradition

Jesus noted the power struggles of his time and responded to them. We know of him through the Gospels. They are a collection of sayings and actions of Jesus (culminating in the consecutive account of the last days of his life in Jerusalem) which served preachers as they sought to win people to faith in him. The Gospels were composed between forty (Mark) and seventy (John) years after the events and have retained what the communities which had come into being in the meantime regarded as worth handing down and useful for their missionary purposes.

The present-day historian who wants to know what happened around the year 30 CE can infer much from this preaching material. Often it is not easy to separate the sober facts clearly from the colouring given to them by the preachers, colouring which is associated with their purpose. Argument over this among scholars is controversial and exciting. But we are not asking here what really happened around the year 30 and how it happened, but as earlier in the case of Moses what religious conclusions the authors of the Gospels drew for themselves from the life and work of Jesus. We are not asking what Jesus' ministry was really like, but what effect he had on those who wrote the Gospels. What did they take over from Jesus in order to meet the challenges of their lives? What kind of guidance, correction and strengthening did they receive through him? Can we discover a further step in the manifestation of God in their comments on Jesus?

What impressed Christians about the message and ministry of Jesus one or two generations after his death and resurrection was his understanding of God and the consequences that this had for human life. His God is the God of the Bible, as he shows himself in the stories about Abraham and Moses, in the prophets, in the Book of Job and the Psalms. Jesus takes his stand on the ground of Moses' message: 'The one God has chosen you to bear witness to him.'

He takes up the call of the prophets to show justice to the weak: 'Do not be served, but serve!'

The new heart of which Jeremiah and Ezekiel spoke is possible now, as God is not merely in the future, but is among you here and now.

To the God of the Psalms he says, 'Father, if you will, take this cup of suffering from me; but let not my will but yours be done.'

Job was 'righteous and godfearing, and shunned evil', but he was so preoccupied with himself that he had no eye for his visitors. It was only God's storm which opened his eyes so that he could help them. Jesus commended this eye for the opportunity to offer positive support: only if you become like children will you have any experience which can enrich you. The man from Samaria (Luke 10), who from the Jewish perspective belonged to a misguided religious group, had this open eye. The priest and the Levite – righteous, godfearing men like Job – were concerned above all with their own affairs and passed over the opportunity that lay by the wayside to become involved as instruments of the good and experience the joy of 'eternal life'.

Jesus wanted this understanding of God to shape everyday life. He proclaimed it as an itinerant rabbi, often in parables, teaching and conversations. He militantly supported it to the point of marching on Jerusalem, the religious and political centre. Here a dispute broke out over two themes which were a preoccupation in the religious and therefore also in the public life of the time: the expectations of salvation which had arisen since Daniel, and the Torah, God's instruction, his commandment.

2. *Jesus' attitude to God's commandment: An unconditional concern for men and women*

Jesus affirmed the prescriptions of the Torah in so far as they called for responsibility before God and towards other men and women; but if they no longer helped human relationships to flourish, as in the case of sabbath observance, they were no longer binding. He commented on the right use of the law by combining two old biblical commandments (Deuteronomy 6 and Leviticus 19): 'You shall love the Lord your God with all your heart and all your soul and all your strength, and your neighbour as yourself.' All Jesus' instructions which are concerned with specific areas of life elucidate this basic commandment.

Men and women find peace with God and with themselves when they trust in his guidance: 'Your will be done.' They find peace with those they do not easily get on with by coming to meet them – 'If you offer a sacrifice at the altar, first go and reconcile yourself with your brother' – and by being responsible for seeing that their opponents grow and flourish: 'Love your enemies' (Matthew 5). With this demand Jesus points to God's attitude towards the 'wicked'. God gives them the same as the 'good': sun and rain, so that they can grow. God, who himself embodies the goal of humankind, and whom Jesus remarkably calls 'perfect', is interested that both those who have progressed and those who have been left behind should arrive at their goal and achieve perfection: therefore he offers them the chance to grow. Jesus says: 'Help people to grow; that is what you too should do as children of God.'

Jesus was concerned for the outcasts of society, the 'publicans and sinners'. In this way he demonstrated the style of the relationships which prevail in the community of the perfect – in the kingdom of God. It is open to the unattractive, so that they too can grow. It is no longer characterized by blamelessness in respect of the moral law, but by readiness to allow oneself to be disturbed by others who need support in growing.

Gifts are not there for thoughtless consumption but are put at our disposal to be used rightly: 'Give us today our daily bread.' In particular, Jesus exclaimed to the privileged, 'Woe to you rich, you have your comfort.'

God's call often reaches us more directly in prayer than by way of legalistic obedience: 'God, be gracious to me a sinner.'

Partners for life are not there to exploit one another but to grow towards one another and with one another: 'Anyone who looks lustfully at a woman has already committed adultery with her in his heart.'

Jesus sets the attitude of faith over against disappointments: 'Do not fear, only believe.'

If people expose themselves to the healing power which transcends their limited capacities they will experience this healing power and be healed: 'Ask and it will be given to you; seek and you will find; knock and it will be opened to you.'

3. Jesus' attitude to the expectation of salvation: The kingdom of God is possible today

Expectations of salvation in Jesus' day were directed partially towards liberation from Roman rule and Jewish influence in world politics, and partly towards a state of repose and untroubled happiness in the world beyond. At all events, conditions were to be more favourable than they were then: less strenuous, disappointing and questionable.

What the authors of the Gospels remembered about Jesus' reaction to this is both clear and surprising. Their interest was concentrated on the account of the week of Jesus' conflict, suffering, death and exaltation during the national celebration which recalled the people's liberation from the Egyptian yoke. What the Gospels report in addition reads like a somewhat extended introduction to these events in Jerusalem. They are what counts. In order that the introduction and the main part shall be properly understood by the reader, Mark and Matthew preface their accounts of the whole story with a saying of Jesus: 'The kingdom of God is at hand; repent, change.'

Jesus rejects the way of the militant Zealots, who as underground fighters wanted to do away with Roman rule. And what was his attitude to the hopes of salvation in apocalyptic literature? He uses the same language, but gives it a different, more urgent, content with his call to conversion: 'There is good fortune for you now, not in the future but today. However, it depends on your readiness to repent. The kingdom of God is possible for you today, because God's call goes out to you today - through me.' All that Jesus said is an application of this statement. Jesus makes use of the language of hope which was on everyone's lips and speaks of the 'kingdom of God'. But how does he interpret it? He too proclaims the imminence of a new time. But he does not allow his gaze to be directed away from the constraints of the present to trouble-free future conditions; on the contrary, he takes hold of people and puts them in the present. His message of the future makes a claim on people today: you must already live now on the basis of your great possibilities; you must change now. Men and women must accept the kingdom of God in the present with their whole existence. Believers do not have the kingdom of God dawning only for themselves, but also for others. That is the meaning of sayings like those about the salt, the better righteousness, loving one's enemies. Jesus says: a solution to all your needs is possible; but first seek contact with God, listen to his call and follow him by being changed – 'and all the things you need will be yours as well'.

4. *Jesus' consciousness of his mission: The authority of the one sent by God*

Jesus asserted that he was of decisive importance, for the call of God reached people through him and his activity. This consciousness of his mission made it clear that through him God's will came to men and women in a comprehensive way now – not later. He was prepared to sacrifice himself completely for others and required the same thing of them in return. That was his understanding of the call of God, rooted in the old prophetic message. This call brought the expected new time; the new time was there if the call was heard and followed. It was present in Jesus' words and actions. So he understood himself as the anointed of God, as the prophet expected in the end time. Jesus read from Isaiah 61 in the synagogue of his home town, Nazareth: 'The Spirit of God is upon me because he has anointed me to proclaim the good news to the poor...' He then put the book aside and said: 'Today this word of scripture is fulfilled in your ears' (Luke 4).

Jesus' consciousness of his mission is expressed in the accounts of his days in Jerusalem. His claim that 'God's kingdom present through me and my call is both a gift and a task' tones down the value of tradition and future hopes. In this way the position of the leaders in Jerusalem was shaken. For they were the ones who were responsible for both. His consciousness of who he was put their efforts in question, so they had to try to get rid of him. They did it through Pilate, who had Jesus executed as a messianic disturber of the peace and thus as an enemy of the Roman empire.

The authority with which Jesus announces the imminence of the rule of God means that the shift in the ages has already come about. 'Blessed are you poor, for the kingdom of God is yours. Blessed are those who beg for God's spirit, for the kingdom of God belongs to them. Blessed are those who are persecuted for the sake of righteousness, for the kingdom of heaven belongs to them.' When John the Baptist sent to ask him, 'Are you the anointed one who is to come or should we wait for someone else?', Jesus replied: 'The blind see and the lame walk and the poor have the good news proclaimed: good for the one who does not take offence at me!' God's rule was coming about in what Jesus said and did, and it would not be experienced by the pious who were well prepared for later but by those who were not prepared, those who had been marginalized at the periphery of society, the tax-collectors and sinners, those who were not insured for the future by any kind of possession, religious or otherwise, but those who in both social and religious terms were beggars.

5. *The call for repentance: God reassures by disturbing people*

God's call for repentance disturbs the human conscience. In modern terms, Jesus' call to people to repent since God's kingdom is now possible might be put like this: 'Life is for those who are ready to be disturbed'. God satisfies, i.e. reassures, by disturbing people. God's peace does not mean conditions which are available for pleasant consumption; rather, this peace makes possible an attitude which allows them to believe in a meaning for life even if the immediate conditions are rather unsatisfactory. The peace, happiness, salvation that God holds ready is the expression of a love which has been freed for complete surrender. It is not constrained either by bad experiences or by anxiety for the future. It knows these constricting bonds, but it grapples with them. In religious terms, it is grasped by the loving will of God. To put it simply, it is glad to be used as the instrument of the good, even in adverse circumstances.

Jesus was not unaware that his claim to embody God's presence would bring him into difficulties with the religious authorities and therefore under political pressure. The fate of John the Baptist was a warning example. But it was impossible for him to evade this task. It would have meant betraying himself.

Jesus' resolve to go to Jerusalem introduces the turning point in his life. It was important for him to proclaim the message of conversion in the religious centre, too. There he wanted to summon people to decision, and his disciples hoped that the kingdom of God as they understood it would appear.

With his pilgrimage to the temple in Jerusalem Jesus sought a decision. On his entry he was jubilantly celebrated as God's anointed and proclaimed that with his call the kingdom of God was dawning and the time of decision was here. That was a declaration of war on the religious leaders, and in the temple he attacked church practices which prevented people from being disturbed by God (Matthew 21).

6. *The misunderstanding: 'We hoped that he would redeem Israel'*

What the disciples expected of Jesus was that he would free the people from foreign rule or usher in the end of this confused world by a miraculous divine judgment in which the righteous would be transported to a state of undisturbed happiness. However, this expectation was not met by Jesus' claim that with his call to salvation the expected salvation of God had dawned. Only after Easter were the disciples to understand his proclamation.

Attacked by his opponents and misunderstood by those who were faithful to him, Jesus went his lonely way in obedience to inner necessity. His disciples had been deeply moved by him; his spell held them captive; his compelling power proved irresistible. But they followed without being able to say precisely why. He was their master, but to understand him only partially was to misunderstand him. They expected something of him for themselves, but the message was: God expects decision from you; with my mission God's power is there once for all as summons and help. As for the kingdom of God that you long for, you do not need to wait for anything else; make use of the gift by taking on today's task; I lead you in living out this dedication to God; follow me.

In the course of his life Jesus had, as the Letter to the Hebrews puts it, 'learned' that a life under the claim of the presence of the kingdom of God leads to suffering. Suffering makes God's kingdom concrete. It helps others. In this way he takes up Second Isaiah's message about the constructive power of unmerited suffering on the part of God's messenger.

The disciples of Jesus did not understand any of this in his lifetime. They did not expect from him strength for their souls so much as less oppressive conditions: 'We hoped that he would redeem Israel', they said on the road to Emmaus after his death. When on Good Friday they could no longer get hold of him, they had lost their point of contact. They were confused and stripped of their illusions. Shamed before themselves and their circle of acquaintances, they crept back to their native villages and disappeared from public view.

7. *Jesus' basic concern: self-development in partnership*

We now know that the disciples were pulled out of their collapse by the events between Easter and Pentecost. Before we turn to these we should ask: what new things does the earthly career of the prophet from Nazareth sent by God tell us about the aim of human life?

Jesus did not point out a different way to God from that which had been handed down to him in his Bible. He did not put forward anything new as God's claim; but he stressed the value of this claim for human coming of age.

The change which Jesus calls for as a necessary accompaniment to the rule of God does not lead to narrowness but to self-discovery. Jesus calls on people to emerge from their shells, to lay open their innermost heart, to develop.

Jesus' answer to the questions about God's law and the expectation of salvation that are put to him is: you can get beyond the external fulfilment of the commandment and encounter the one who commands: he leads you to repentance – away from waiting for things to change. In that way you will be a superior force capable of creative action in this absurd world by creating community.

Just as the God of Moses called the Hebrews to do more than just reproduce themselves, namely to bear witness to him before the world by acting in partnership, so too Jesus calls men and women to use their gifts in service and not just consume them. That is disturbing and therefore helpful. A lesser offer by God would remain below the level of the biblical aim of turning to one's fellow human beings, including one's enemies.

God shows his love and grace – nowadays we would say his interest in men and women – by giving them a concern for community. Jesus' basic concern is for partnership, which usually can only be achieved painfully. But the result is happiness, salvation, our common goal.

If God's mercy is not understood as this kind of participation in responsible action, it leads to a superficial humanity which used to be called 'spiritual death'. God's mercy then comes to grief on cheap grace – men and women do not grow but remain infantile, even as so-called adults. Jesus wants to preserve people from that. He knows that the goal of life is the development of a healed self which succeeds in co-operating with others even in difficult circumstances.

IV | The Origin of Christian Faith

1. Easter and Pentecost: The discovery of a new way of life

It is a historical fact that the Christian faith came into being through the events of the weeks between Easter and Pentecost. What happened then? What did it mean for the disciples?

The men who had been completely shattered by what happened on Good Friday, and who had crept back to their homes in the country, emerged in public seven weeks later in such excitement that they were thought to be drunk. From intimidated, anxious individuals they had turned into a convinced band of militants who, specifically referring to the defeat of their master Jesus, invited the rest of the world to join them in their happy conviction that the defeat of their master had not been a demonstration of the inadequacy of his aims and his power but the necessary transitional stage to a new quality of life. This was now accessible to anyone. All that had previously been felt to be a hindrance to successful personal development – personal failure and undeserved fate – could be experienced as whole, fulfilled, i.e. eternal life; not just in a future society of freedom, equality and brother/sisterhood or in a heavenly world beyond, in freedom from burdens, but already in the midst of disquieting circumstances. The condition was that one had to enter the sphere of influence of this crucified man who had been raised to eternal, fulfilled existence. In other words, one had to be baptized in his name and then allow one's everyday life to be guided by him. That was the discovery of a new living space. These people were apparently fanatics, or else the pioneers in a new way of life.

The appearances of the risen Christ: Light over the cross

What had brought about this change in them? They replied that their crucified master, a public outcast, had appeared to them as a powerful influence. The earliest account of this is in a letter of Paul. He was originally an opponent of the Christians, but about three years after Jesus' death he had an unexpected encounter with Jesus as a bright, blinding light. Jesus had said to him, 'I am Jesus whom you are persecuting; but from now on you are in my service: go and open the eyes of the Gentiles so that they may come out of darkness into the true light.'

In the year 55 CE Paul wrote to his congregation in Corinth about the experiences of the disciples between Easter and Pentecost and about his own encounter with Christ: 'It was reported to me that Christ, the Risen One, appeared to Peter, then to the Twelve. After that he appeared to more than 500 brothers at one time, most of whom are still alive, though some have fallen asleep. Then he appeared to James, then to all the apostles. Last of all, as to a "latecomer", he also appeared to me.' In his letter to the Galatians Paul said: 'When it pleased God to reveal his Son to me that I might proclaim him through the gospel among the Gentiles, I did not confer with anyone about my experience... but only about three years later I came to Jerusalem to visit Peter. I stayed there for two weeks and also met James the brother of the Lord.' At that time Peter and James attached the same value to the encounter which Paul had with Jesus before Damascus as that of the appearance of the Risen Christ to them. Jesus' death on Golgotha and his burial were facts which could have been registered in the local records, but the appearances of the Risen Christ to his followers in Galilee, Jerusalem and Damascus were not like that. The first Christians did not say anything to Paul about an empty tomb. These appearances were not events which could be documented in the public world but gifts of God – miracles – to the host of believers through which a particular interpretation of the death of their master was communicated to them. His death was not the end of his activity but the necessary transition to a powerful, eternal activity.

The significance of the Easter events: Renewal through the venture of trust

Even someone who was not there at the same time can also see Jesus' death as a transition, in which case he or she stands in line with those who experienced the appearances at Easter and Pentecost two thousand years ago. The renewal that one experiences is the same as that which the disciples experienced. Now as then the master's death, as a transition to a liberated, 'eternal' activity, leads to a new attitude to failure and guilt and to deliverance from the bonds of a destiny into which one has been thrown.

Jesus could not have known that this victory would follow his defeat on Good Friday. People nowadays know more than Jesus knew on Good Friday. They know that at Easter the disciples were given faith in the saving efficacy of Jesus' death on the cross.

God is the one invisible, all-embracing and therefore incomprehensible, indeed uncanny, power which makes us tremble. This power takes people in its grasp even when they think they have a grasp on themselves. It shows them their limitations. It forces them to live and gives them a longing for love; but is it regularly fulfilled? It gives them ideas and the power to put them into action, and at the same time has them caught up in the torment of tragic entanglement. God is the power beyond life which has a mysterious effect in this world. Even before Jesus, there were voices of those – Jeremiah, Second Isaiah, some Psalms, Job – who felt attracted by God despite his unfathomable and sometimes dark being and hoped in confidence for good things from him.

Those who believe in the crucified Jesus who has been exalted expect this God to lead them on a way worth living. Looking confidently at what happened to Jesus in Galilee and Jerusalem and to Paul on the road to Damascus, they venture to see in the constraints of life the possibility of enrichment and fulfilment. So they call him God's Son, the mediator between them and the mysterious God. In this way believers express what Christ means for them and what they let him do for them. It is an expression of their gratitude that their life contains meaning and direction in an uncanny, absurd world because of him.

Holy Spirit: the new awareness

A new, comprehensive aim in life is offered in the biblical writings, which ennobles suffering. One can affirm or reject this goal. To believe in the effective power of the crucified one – which is what exaltation or resurrection means – is to bear witness to the newly acquired awareness of being able to grow through the impact of suffering; so this pressure can be accepted as the guidance of God. This new awareness is called Holy Spirit. It was given to the disciples at Pentecost and is also given today to those who are open to it. The new consciousness expectantly says yes to the frustration of its own efforts. The Lord's Prayer says 'Thy – not my – will be done'.

The religion of the cross: suffering as a productive force

The pressure of suffering is not a pleasant experience. It does not make people happy, but disturbs them. One may hope that a blessing will follow from it. But it is impossible to know beforehand what this will look like and whether it will happen. The suffering consists in grievous pain. Believers think that this is meaningful, but the particular form which suffering takes is certainly not what they would have liked. What is experienced first and painfully is separation from accustomed things, people and hopes on which the believer depends. He or she does not know when and how a different kind of life will be made possible as a result of the loss. A look at some historical catastrophes may illustrate this well.

When the inhabitants of Jerusalem were led away from their homeland by the Babylonians after the destruction of their city, they sat by the waters of Babylon and wept. They could have had no inkling that with the help of the Second Isaiah their belief in God would lose its nationalistic limitations there and that a new way of life woul be given to the world with Psalm 73. This was the hour in which a mature optimism, regardless of success, was born.

When Roman culture collapsed in the barbarian invasions, for many people this was not only a material but also a spiritual catastrophe. When Alaric's Goths plundered the villas of Rome and Geiseric's Vandals ravaged Africa, it seemed pointless to plan a life which promised a future. 'Is nihilism our destiny? Does it still make sense to believe in God?', the pious asked their spiritual leaders. Augustine replied, 'Yes, certainly. Granted, what is happening now does not point to the preservation of the existing order but to a change, indeed a collapse. But what is expected of you is most meaningful. You certainly cannot remain what you were and as you were. Your fate is like that of the olive in the olive press. It squeezes you. But you have a choice as to whether you come out as the husk, mere cellulose, or as oil, which is urgently needed.'

And what did come out? When Roman culture, which was dependent on slave labour, came to an end, a new culture arose out of the 'Pray and work' of the cloister. Its power lay in service rather than in rule and obedience. The principle 'What counts is work and prayer' opened up the way to the culture of a brotherly and sisterly relationship which did not fall perfect from heaven overnight (think of serfdom in the Middle Ages and piecework in modern times); we are still in the process of shaping it. But a new possibility of co-operation had been born: human value no longer lies in birth or power, but in work and service.

The Thirty Years' War in the seventeenth century brought devastation and unspeakable suffering to Central Europe, but it opened the way to something that was new and extremely important: tolerance instead of a narrow dogmatic attitude. Since then we have come to realize that other people have the same rights as we do to be themselves, in different ways from us. We can put up with one another and co-operate, despite the ongoing existence of differences. Granted, this tolerance has not been achieved completely, but its ideal is striking.

No one who experienced these catastrophes would have felt that such developments were possible. Even the crucifixion of Jesus had had a different result from what Jesus had planned: no religious reform of his people, nor even a new – messianic – age, but a new, worldwide way of life, the religion of the cross. If they are there at all, the positive results of terrifying losses are only recognized in retrospect and are always different from what was imagined and expected.

Our hope in the midst of the pressures of suffering is to follow Christ's example and 'learn obedience by suffering' (Hebrews 5), i.e. accept the way of the cross. The Christ who comes to us is the cross which comes to us. Only those who are painfully born anew, who die like the grain of wheat or are pruned like the vine by the vintner's knife bring forth the fruit which creates community (Galatians 5), that which is completely new (Revelation 21).

The trust in the future which is based on Easter brings confidence, but what that future will look like is not known. The tension of the unknown outcome remains, and its resolution is not yet in view. Trust in the one who achieved victory through the cross supplies strength, but only as hope. The one who trusts can rejoice – but with patience.

2. *Paul*

His life

Paul, too, had to face this problem and solved it for himself. About thirty years lie between his experience before Damascus and his death in Rome. We know where he had been during the first half of this time: first of all in Damascus and in Transjordan (the present kingdom of Jordan), for a short time in Jerusalem with Peter and James the brother of Jesus, and then in his home area of Cilicia in Asia Minor and in Syria (with Antioch, where the supporters of Jesus were called Christians for the first time). We do not know the shape of his activity in these first years. He made tents for a living. During his thirty 'Christian' years he was unmarried. We do not know whether he was married earlier, but that is improbable. The year 48 brought an important shift in his missionary activity. He travelled to Jerusalem in order to clarify with the central community there the question of the significance of the Jewish law in the mission among non-Jews. He felt that he had been called to that.

We are well informed about the subsequent period. These were years of intensive activity as a travelling preacher, founding communities in Asia Minor (Galatia, Cyprus and

Ephesus) and Greece (Philippi, Thessalonica and Corinth). On a third visit to Jerusalem in 56 Paul was taken into Roman custody because of threatening Jewish attacks and escorted to Caesarea on the coast. When after a two-year imprisonment the Roman adminstration was making no arrangements to bring his case to trial and a decision – the Jewish accusation related to causing religious and political unrest – as a Roman citizen he appealed to the imperial court in Rome and was taken there by ship. After a shipwreck off Malta in which the escort and passengers were saved, and his arrival in Rome, he spent two further years under open arrest in Rome. He was then probably executed as a troublemaker under Nero, but we have no exact information about his death.

Paul grew up in the non-Jewish culture of the university city of Tarsus. He then studied theology – biblical monotheism – in Jerusalem, the spiritual centre of Judaism. He was one of the group of Pharisees and therefore took the faith particularly seriously; as a diaspora Jew who spoke Greek he was especially concerned to communicate the nature and the moral weight of the Jewish idea of God to his Hellenistic contemporaries. He was enabled to do this by a spiritual sensitivity and alertness which present-day student pastors need in order to be understood by those whom they seek to bring closer to God.

The Damascus experience

In making this effort Paul came up against rivalry from the disciples of Jesus which irritated him in two respects.

1. For a practising Jew the Torah was the divine revelation of the meaning of life, the basis of life. As the message of the one God it was a form of his grace. Grateful obedience to it was the only acceptable reaction. But the disciples of Jesus said that the author of the Torah was more important than the book. They did not reject it as the command to love

God and neighbour, but they did not keep to the letter of it. That was particularly evident in their indifference towards some cultic rituals.

2. The followers of Jesus saw Jesus' failure as the way through to a healthy human attitude towards the challenges of life. But where did that leave being concerned for the good? Were the tax-collectors and sinners, 'those in the shadows', to be nearer to God than the observant Jews who bore their burdens of the law? Paul had learned otherwise.

Then, around three years after the death of Jesus, his appearance on the road to Damascus convinced Paul that this crucified man was the expected saviour who makes people whole – not just the Jews but all people; the only condition of acquiring health was to believe in Jesus' cross as the way by which we encounter the power of the living God and to live as Jesus had done, namely by letting oneself be crucified. 'Anyone who belongs to Christ crucifies his self with its passions and desires' (Galatians 5; also Romans 6; Galatians 2).

The end of the law

Paul explained in Galatians that it was unnecessary to observe the Jewish law in order to receive divine salvation and have a right aim in life; it could even be a hindrance. His argument went like this. Before God opened up the new way to himself through Jesus Christ, we were shut up in the prison of the law. The law kept us under strict supervision. That lasted until the coming of Christ – crucified and risen. For through trust in him we are to get straight with God. That is what has happened. Therefore we are no longer under the law, the Torah. You are all God's children because God has opened up the way of trust to you through Jesus Christ. If you have put yourself under his influence through baptism you have as it were slipped into his skin. Therefore it no longer matters before God who or what we are – Jew or

Gentile, slave or free, man or woman – we have all obtained through Jesus Christ the same chance for a meaningful life.

For Paul, with the coming of the crucified and exalted Jesus the time longed for by the biblical patriarchs had dawned, with the possibility of leading a life of obedient surrender to God and of all-embracing love for one's fellow human beings. In so far as the law of God was a help towards 'obedience to the faith', i.e. to a bond with the one who gave it, one experienced liberation. But to the degree that it seduced one into being content with merely fulfilling it or even referring to its fulfilment – especially if no distinction were made between the moral commandments and cultic-ritual commandments – this law amounted to a constraint which did not set one free for others. Paul fought for this insight in his communities and also helped to establish it at his meeting with the apostles in Jerusalem. In this way the possibility was opened up for Jewish monotheistic faith to organize itself as a world religion. Without liberation from the Jewish ritual law the Christian community would have remained a sect within Judaism.

Jesus had not yet explicitly been faced with this question. He had worked within the Jewish sphere. His daily struggle was that his fellow countrymen should have a right relationship to God. But when non-Jews approached him, like the Roman officer who asked him for help for his soldiers, and the woman from Tyre who made a request about her daughter, he demonstrated to them the power of the one God of Israel which he himself embodied, without their having to become Jews. Therefore Paul's activity was wholly along the lines of that of Jesus.

Hope for the perfect world

Paul also clarified the meaning of the Christian hope. The issue was the imminent coming, the return, of Christ as judge and redeemer of the world.

After his meeting with the apostles in Jerusalem, Paul visited communities in Asia Minor with a friend called Silas and a young man called Timothy. At Troas they decided to go over to Europe. They arrived at Philippi, where they landed up in prison, but there Paul was able to found a community which he always remembered with affection. He began a letter to it some years later with the words, 'Whenever I think of you I thank my God that you have accepted the good news and that it is at work among you from the first days up to now. That always fills me with joy. I am quite certain that God will complete what he has begun in you until the coming of Jesus Christ.'

'Until the coming of Jesus Christ!' Although around twenty years had already passed since Jesus' resurrection, there was a strong expectation in the Jesus communities that the day of his return to judge the world was imminent. Paul shared this expectation. From Philippi he continued to Thessalonica, where he depicted the imminent end of the world in vivid colours: 'The Lord will descend from heaven with a cry of command, with the archangel's call, and with the sound of the trumpet of God; the dead in Christ will rise first, then afterwards we who are still alive will be taken with them on clouds to the Lord in the air and so we shall be always with him.'

These assertions proved to be dangerous. The Jews in Thessalonica, outraged by the statement that a crucified man was the expected bringer of salvation, used Paul's talk of the coming kingdom of Christ to accuse him of high treason before the authorities and managed to get the missionaries expelled from the city. They even pursued them to the next place and agitated against them there. Silas disappeared into the underground and Paul was sent on to Athens as quickly as possible by his hosts. While he was waiting for Silas there he attempted to interest the educated Greeks in Jesus and his role as the Risen Christ. But as soon as he spoke of his conviction about the return of the judge of the world from the realm of the dead, people began to laugh at him. So he went on to Corinth to wait for the others. Timothy, whom he had meanwhile ordered to Thessalonica to see that everything was all right there, brought positive news that the community was ready to resist. Paul drew new hope from this and wrote to the community to tell them how much this news had delighted him.

Soon, however, disturbing reports reached him. The notion of the return of Christ to end the world in power and glory had so excited the community that some members had given up their regular work and were sitting around waiting for the end. The community was being talked about. So Paul wrote them a short, hasty letter: 'Do not let yourselves be too quickly confused or terrified by the assertion that the day of the Lord's return is close at hand. Before the return of Christ the adversary will come and usher in the great apostasy from God.'

The idea that God's adversary, later called the Antichrist, has to precede the appearance of the saviour, stems from the Judaism of the time, and Christians liked to use it to explain the delay in the expected return of Jesus. They wanted to hold on to this expectation as long as possible; it was less exciting to look forward to the salvation of the future kingdom than already to live a disciplined life in the present.

The tendency to look to the future return of Christ for everything finds its most marked expression in the New Testament in the Revelation of John. This book falls short of the message of the earthly Jesus, the Easter faith of the disciples and Paul's Damascus experience. The concern of believers is shifted from the present to the future.

Paul initially used the idea of God's adversary to dampen down the excitement in Thessalonica, but it did not satisfy him. He thought again about the question why the Lord had still not returned after twenty years, and came to the conclusion that he should hold firm to the expectation of his return; however, through Christ's death and resurrection sins had already been forgiven, and that was the essential thing. His answer points in the same direction as Jesus' instructions about the right way for men and women to live in the world.

Paul stressed that Christ is already there. 'If anyone has come within the sphere of influence of Christ, he is a new creation: for him the old is past and a new way of life has been opened up.' However, the old powers still oppress us as they always have done; the new element, the power of the resurrection, is at work only in the community which bears the cross. The community of Christ is the home of the Spirit of the Lord in the midst of the old structures and is his active instrument in the world; it is his body. The members of this organism bear witness with their bodies to the love of God, the grace of Christ and the fellowship of the Holy Spirit. The death and resurrection of Jesus open up the new possibility of a creative life free from anxiety. People long for it to be realized. That is the meaning of the idea of the end of time, of its consummation in the return of Christ as judge. People put themselves under the judgment without hiding away. Judgment makes it possible to enter into the kingdom of heaven, to breathe freely and without constraint. The way in is through the narrow door, in other words, by means of the frustrations that one undergoes. The consummation is not a guaranteed possession, but a life experienced in the community which the judgment has freed from anxiety. The community is the place in this often confused world where the power of Christ establishes its renewing force. In it his power is manifest. The community of believers, those who bear the cross, is the answer to the question how there can be credible redemption in a world which is still waiting for its final redemption.

The traditional modes of thought and conduct still seek to govern believers; but they are no longer all that governs them. A new possibility can be grasped: believers can join in bearing Jesus' cross. The world is not yet new, but the new becomes visible in the world as a community bearing the cross. The cross is not done away with by the resurrection, but seen as a way through to salvation, which will show itself in the hoped-for consummation.

This will not correspond to the expectations and notions of the people with the new awareness: 'We live in faith and not by sight.' But it will offer an extended, comprehensive possibility of life; believers may hope for it. Therefore Paul calls 'dying' a 'gain'. 'Then we shall be ever with the Lord.' He expects a communion with the one to whom he knows that he himself already belongs which is no longer hindered by weakness and sin. For him, communion with Christ means belonging to the community which is going forward to its consummation. In that community it is possible to grow and mature together. Even there the goal has not yet been reached; but the community goes towards it in expectation. Paul describes this confident expectation of the consummation as hope. It does not give a foretaste of a healed world in which all people may feel good, but it does strengthen the faith of the community which bears witness to the new consciousness made possible by Christ.

3. *The Gospels: A call to discipleship*

Paul achieved his aim. The Christians no longer avoided their daily tasks but reflected on how they had to live as believers in the world as it was. For that, however, they needed information about Jesus' earthly life which they could use as a call to follow their Lord in the present.

The first three Gospels met this need for information: the Gospel of Mark with its account of what Jesus did; the Gospel of Matthew with the Sermon on the Mount, the new law of love for the citizens of the kingdom of God; and the Gospel of Luke with Jesus as the model of life as God wills it.

John in his Gospel takes Paul's standpoint as his basis. He

writes: 'God so loved the world that he gave his only Son that all who believe in him should live, should not be lost, but have eternal life...' 'Anyone who trusts in the Son of God will not be condemned. But anyone who does not trust in him is condemned already.' He makes Jesus say: 'Anyone who hears my word and trusts the one who sent me has eternal life. He is not condemned, but has already been rescued from the sphere of death (where he is) into the sphere of life (where he is used to bring forth fruit).' 'He brings forth fruit like the grain of wheat that falls into the ground.' The evangelist explains that those who trust will not just be given salvation in the future, but already now. Those who trust find their problems answered in the cross and resurrection of Jesus: he lives in union with all brothers and sisters who have the same awareness and brings them peace.

4. *Jews and Christians: the common task*

Without the Easter visions, Jesus' message is a call like that of the Second Isaiah about the suffering messenger of God who brings salvation, or like the message of the book of Job about the liberation of the pious ego from itself. However, things did not stop at Easter. What did the exaltation of Jesus at Easter, Pentecost and before Damascus mean for the disciples? They experienced the rise of a community which was held together by the message about bringing forth fruit by dying, and which became a new factor in the cultural development of the world.

For centuries Moses, the prophets, Job and the Psalmists proclaimed to the people of their time the message of coming alive by allowing oneself to be disturbed – as later did Jesus, Paul and the first Christians. The God of the Bible had been concerned with all men and women from the beginning. However, the political and cultural unification of the Mediterranean at the beginning of our era facilitated the acceptance of the message, as was to emerge in the extension of the Christian communities.

Could the world-wide cultural interchange in our day lead to the Jewish-Christian understanding of human nature increasingly being put in question by the conviction that everything – whether good or evil – is a single movement into which we are caught up without being able to direct it? This understanding of the world and humankind is put forward in the philosophy of Eastern Asia and Western science.

In the face of this challenge, theoretical questions like whether Jesus is the expected messiah and whether the church has taken the place of the synagogue lose their importance. The question which the Far-Eastern and scientific world-view puts to the biblical tradition is whether it makes sense to rely on a power to which (or to whom) human beings are prepared to be responsible. Does this sense of responsibility give them such a state of independence that, although being woven into the causality of the world, they can still look at it from a distance? Both Jews and Christians are called today to explain clearly the root and aim of their common responsibility. This task makes irrelevant the traditional Christian claim of religious superiority which has encouraged pogroms since the Middle Ages and has offered moral support to genocide in Germany. It opens our eyes to the discovery of God in the Old Testament. In a world threatened with despair, even the message of the Bible before Jesus offers freedom from anxiety and can free men and women to do what God wills in a contradictory world.

PART TWO

Belief in God Today

1. *The discovery of God as a challenge to growth*

Our way through the history of biblical religion has shown that from the time of Moses 'God' was discovered step by step as a power which challenges people to grow. If they accept the challenge, they are led to the community of those who bear the cross. This makes it possible for them to experience joy in a contradictory world by furthering community life. A systematic look at this discovery should finally establish the character of the biblical offer.

Adam and Eve, being a part of nature in the garden of Eden, have no awareness of personal identity. But they wake up. The self with its critical consciousness is stirred (Gen.2.3). Human beings recognize their potentialities and become aware of their capacity to make a free choice between them, and thus also to make wrong decisions. Harmony with nature is interrupted. Humankind starts out towards individuation and the distresses of alienation; in other words, into history. The myth of the departure from paradise reports the awakening of human beings to themselves. By coming to grips with the natural and human environment with which they are confronted, men and women progress towards self-development.

In the Bible men and women are not sedentary; they travel. Abraham shakes off the bonds of his origins (Genesis 12). He forsakes his clan and leaves his past behind him, taking responsibility for himself and making his mark on history. Freedom and independence are required for influence in history. The significance of human self-development is that men and women gain the freedom to make their mark on history.

Israel gives up its protected but constricted existence in Egypt (Exodus 1-14). It frees itself from social and political tutelage to follow the dangerous course of self-development and to determine its own fate. First of all it is still through obedience to the authority of Yahweh, about which no questions are asked, that Israel becomes socially and politically free.

However, the making of the covenant with the law given to Moses on Sinai (Exodus 19-20), along with the prophets, marks a further step in self-development. 'You shall love others – and in that way you will find your identity' (Leviticus 19). 'Seek good and not evil, that you may live' (Amos 5). Instead of being subordinated to an authority without asking why, men and women develop convictions and principles in order to remain true to themselves. God comes to an agreement with humankind about the principles of morality, which bind God as well. Morality must have a basis in rationality. It must satisfy our desire for understanding. The spiritual power of the teacher replaces the natural power of the father and the social power of the ruler. People are freed from the image of God as an autocrat. Authorities which keep people from hearing the call for the next step in being concerned for others hinder their own growth and that of the community. They are fetters from which one must be freed.

All individuals are brothers and sisters and should feel responsible even for their enemies (Exod. 23; Matthew 5; 25). Why? Not just for the sake of others but for their own sakes, too. Something new should grow between them: brotherly and sisterly relations. People must be freed from the ties of experiences, particularly those they have of their adversaries. Certainly bad experiences are a warning to take care, but a fixation on the past limits the wealth of possibilities for co-operation. Men and women must become free for a more comprehensive understanding. They must learn to expect that substantial challenges are still to come. Otherwise their chance for attaining solidarity in the community is crippled, and they cease to grow.

The Sermon on the Mount indicates that there can be no relationship with God unless impaired human relationships are restored: 'If you are offering your gift at the altar and there remember that your brother has something against you, go and be reconciled first and then come and offer your gift.' A tax collector who has used his position to exploit the defenceless may celebrate the development of his self with Jesus (Luke 19). He begins to make good the damage he has done by saying: 'If I have cheated anyone, I restore it to him fourfold'; whereupon Jesus replies: 'Today salvation has come to this house.' In present-day language: 'You have seized the opportunity to be yourself. You have broken out of being concerned with having and now you are concerned with being. Now your life has intensity and purpose and you find yourself in the process of a constant growth in quality of life, satisfaction and utter contentment.' Only those who have been violated and damaged can forgive guilt. Therefore if you want to take responsibility for your action you go to the person whom you have hurt and in so doing show yourself to be adult in the eyes of the God who forgives. The way in which you show that you are adult is by not avoiding your opponent but by coming to terms and making good any damage done. If the custom of retribution is part of the religious act, religious services become a testimony that tense relationships have given way to co-operation. For adults, the everyday is present on Sunday.

Once you have made your bed, you have to lie on it. That is also true in the Bible: 'What a person sows, that he will reap' (Galatians 6). The paradise promised by Jesus to the thief on the cross does not spare him civil punishment for his crime. As a result of wrong decisions, especially those which have social consequences, opportunities to do what is necessary may be missed and never return in the same way. Others have to suffer as a result. No divine mercy relieves the wrongdoer of this burden. Forgiveness and grace do not make up for human wrongdoings; they do not preserve the perpetrator and the victim from the consequences of wrong decisions, but make it possible for believers to cope creatively with the consequences. They acknowledge what they have done, make good as far as is necessary and possible, and use their remaining strength with an eye to the future. They repent. The consolation of divine forgiveness lies in the fact that it arouses people to the possibility of making a right decision. This causes them more trouble, but it also brings them more success. That God has mercy on his own means that he helps them to mature.

Behind the image of the grain of wheat which falls into the earth and dies, and only in this way bears fruit (John 12), lies the idea of growth and maturity. Two things are said here. First, that the result of dying is not simply an increase in, an addition to, what exists; it is a transformation: new horizons open up. Moreover the new element does not come into being all at once. The grain is not the wheat used for bread, the form of which is surrendered in a single act, to pass on its power to the flour and bread. Rather, it is seed corn which casts off its protective husks, one after another, in a confident, patient struggle with the powers of the soil, warmth and water and which in a constant struggle with its environment brings forth something new that does not yet exist. The corn progressively becomes free to be what it is destined to be. The self reacts constantly to its environment by developing knowledge and understanding, trust and courage, patience and expectation. The more that it sloughs off the possessions it has inherited, the more clearly it acts as a creative power.

The end of the book of Job shows that people do not become

free for bringing forth fruit by sitting on their laurels, but by being open to change. Job was blameless and upright and avoided evil. There was nothing wrong with that. Nor did the fact that he was aware of this and said so make him an evildoer. However, this relationship with his friends lost its dynamic. They preached at one another; nothing new developed between them. Then Job's eyes were opened and he recognized that as long as he was fixated on his righteousness he had not understood anything of the purpose and guidance of God. Now he could breathe again. He was no longer a captive to his past. He left the citadel of his good deeds for the open field of God's activity, approached his adversaries by praying for them, and thus began to develop.

The hymn in Philippians 2, 'Although Jesus Christ was equal to God he did not cling on to that but emptied himself...' stresses that Jesus did not stick to the possessions that had come down to him; he did not persevere in fruitless stagnation, but let go what he had, affirmed the painful change to the point of renouncing the protective shells of civic honour, recognition by his fellow men and physical life, and so came to have an influence which embraced the world.

Hebrews 5 says of Jesus the Son of God that even he had to learn obedience in the school of suffering during his earthly life. Because he allowed himself to be disturbed, he achieved the goal of maturity 'and being made perfect he became the source of eternal salvation to all who follow him'.

'Eternal salvation' – what does that mean? A well-to-do man belonging to the social élite once asked Jesus: 'What must I do to obtain eternal life?' (Luke 18). Jesus recommended that he should go beyond the usual moral blamelessness of keeping the commandments and leave his interests behind him; disturbed by the problems of other people he was to emerge from the constricting shell of looking after his possessions in order to surrender himself to an unusual extent to those who needed his support and to follow Jesus in this way. Those who help others do not stagnate, but grow out of themselves; they become adults. Their lives become worth living; they have a share in 'eternal salvation'.

In the Bible human beings experience God as a liberating power when they take seriously the ties in which they are involved. These ties bring them up against their limitations. That is sobering; now and then it is also humiliating. It is painful, like being born, but it also opens up a new possibility of living. Jesus once said that only those who are born again can see God's new kingdom (John 3). This picture makes it clear that only those who experience constraints and limitations encounter God's renewing power. This power both makes demands and provides strength and in so doing furthers growth. Anyone who puts up with limitations without self-pity does not go through the narrows without being changed. It is painful, but with the pain there is an indication of growth into a new sphere where it is easier to move and breathe.

Anyone who asks for the coming of the kingdom of God as the Bible teaches, asks for the fellowship of those who help one another to develop a bold, confident and understanding self. This fellowship is the aim for believers. The happiness it provides is not attained in the world beyond. It is not a place which provides compensating justice or an existence without tension. It is and remains a community of people who show concern. In this community we do not remain idle or shout applause but continue to bring forth fruit; and that entails the constant process of dying.

The Bible shows people a course on which they do not

encounter the world in order to change it, but respond to its demands by being changed themselves and thus being woven into it. In so doing they discover themselves. They experience themselves as living beings by not clinging to their possessions but letting them go. Self-development takes place through progressive dying.

The biblical offer is worth noting because it does not leave the ground of what can be experienced. It does not comfort people with that which is invisible and unverifiable, like the possibility of an existence after death. Nor does it compel them to adopt any views about the origin of the world and life. It does not mislead them into diverting their attention from the contradictions of life.

The biblical offer takes human beings and their world seriously. The world is the reality in which men and women have to take their place. The offer trusts that they will shape the world – which is tangible and at everyone's disposal as his or her life between birth and death – in such a way that they can find their fulfilment and joy – their freedom – in it. Liberation is not understood as an overwhelming victory or as redemption received in humility. It is a way: people try to use their opportunities to mature.

2. *A modern view of the biblical understanding of life*

What does the Bible say about the possibilities which confront us, and what tasks does it set us?

It gives the name 'God' to the power which encounters men and women in their consciences. Men and women may be counted on and be regarded as reliable, i.e. personal, and therefore accept the call of this power to make responsible use of all their gifts - their intellectual, financial, sexual, artistic, social, economic and political capabilities, and also their free time. To the degree to which they feel themselves to be bound by this call, other ties cease to be constricting and become the field of activity for creative freedom.

The goal which the divine will sets men and women in their consciences is the one humanity, which includes fellowship with those who are difficult and prove a burden. It is a fellowship in which people do not find their fulfilment apart from others or passing them by, but through deliberate encounter with them.

Disruptions to this course associated with suffering are not an impoverishment of life but are understood as a means of achieving one's aim in life.

This understanding of life nowadays calls for a few explanations.

The meaning of the biblical term 'God'

Human beings need dialogue with God, in other words prayer. What is its value? Do people hear God speaking, making demands on them and encouraging them? May those who pray expect God to accomplish what human beings cannot? Or in the last resort is the person who prays talking only to himself or herself?

The nature of God needs to be clarified if we are to grasp the structure and nature of prayer. Moses worshipped God without images; God is not an object on which one reflects, which one judges, at a distance. It is not a question of there being first God, and secondly people, who thirdly make requests to him. A God who 'is' like a table or a stamp collection is not the God of the Bible. In the biblical understanding God 'exists' in the same way as human beings exist. God does not keep himself to himself but rather turns towards us, saying: 'Adam, where are you? Come here! I have to talk to you.' Whereupon the men and women who hear this call turn from themselves to God (Gen.3; Gen.12; Exod.3; I Kings 19.11; Amos 3.8; 7.15; Isa.6; Jer.1.4-10; Mark 14.36).

When the Bible talks of 'God' it indicates that in a confused world, in which despite their better insights people make life difficult for one another, they nevertheless believe in a meaningful life and feel responsible for helping others. The biblical term 'God' means that people are ready to be challenged and disturbed. By learning not to react with disappointment to disruptions caused by circumstances but creatively, they see the meaning of this world, which is often so contradictory. Life, therefore, is seen in terms of growing courage, composure and insight. 'God' is the guarantee of human value. This guarantee consists in the fact that despite the enigmatic, ambiguous character of the world, it is worth working in it.

The biblical God is not the supreme head of an ideal world lying around our confused human world from where – by orbiting it or even going around in it – he observes people and constantly considers how he can rein them in by commandments and threats or bring some hope to their miserable lot by friendly reassurance. In the Bible God is the reason why human beings, unlike animals, have a conscience: a moral compass which provides them with directional instructions, whether they want them or not. When the Bible speaks of God it speaks of the human sense of responsibility. By 'God' it means the all-embracing power which throws men and women into the riddles of life and gives them a sense that they are called on to master a task which is seemingly impossible to master.

God is not independent of the human sense of responsibility. God is the power who points men and women beyond themselves. This power calls and draws them from outside; it raises them up above the absurd world. It gives them the dignity of being able to distance themselves from this world and to be more than a piece of it (Psalm 8). When the Bible talks of God it regards human beings as the proof that despite everything the world is not absurd but full of meaning. God is the power who draws people on to exist.

People experience God in their inward depths as a call which takes them out of themselves.

In the Bible, those who pray wrestle with this call (Gen.18.20ff.; Jer.20.14-18). They express the way in which they struggle, labour and hope; they unburden themselves (Jer.18.19-23). They realize themselves by entrusting themselves to the all-embracing power (Jeremiah 20.7-13; I Peter 5.7), recognizing the decision of that power as meaningful and looking forward to it (Psalm 37.5,7; 73.21-26; Luke 23.46; II Corinthians 12.7-10). Those who pray in the Bible do not beg, but learn to demolish the life-style that is rooted in the self; they entrust themselves to the power which calls them and turn towards aims that are shared (Matthew 5.23f.). Praying is not an activity separate from other activities, but an attitude which shapes the whole of life. In his novel *A Tale of Two Cities*, Charles Dickens says: 'Prayer comes from the heart and is of no more value than this.' The value of a person's prayer grows to the degree that he or she matures.

The language of faith

If the relationship between men and women and God is a direct one – like that of a couple who share their life – their communication will not be stilted. The language of prayer should not be archaic, nor should it be artificially elevated. It must express lamentation, devotion and expectation. How far may the attitude of biblical faith nowadays be influenced by terms which were customary in the time of Moses, the prophets, Jesus and the apostles?

Within the conceptual horizon of the Bible lie ideas like God's covenant with his people, the Messiah (the anointed one), resurrection and ascension, promise and fulfilment, the atoning sacrifice of the Son of God, purification in the blood of the lamb, the high priesthood of Jesus, Satan and the return of Christ. Hellenistic thought, which was centred on a contrast between the spiritual and the material, then attempted to strengthen the persuasive power of this language by the dogmas of the Trinity, the virgin birth of Jesus and his descent into hell. The Middle Ages added images of the devil, of the pains of hell, purgatory and the joy of paradise; heaven was populated with angels and saints.

There are still people today who are helped by this language to make contact with God and lead a fulfilled life. But those to whom this language does not speak, because it is alien to their education and thought, need not use it. They perhaps experience God's power – stirring them up and renewing them – through biblical concepts like God's guidance, the 'nevertheless' of faith, God's commandment, obedience, following Jesus as disciples, bearing the cross, trusting, hoping, serving, saying 'Your will be done', bringing forth fruit through dying, repentance, being born again, community, judgment, grace, freedom. Expressions from outside the Bible can also be helpful. Anything may be used which brings renewal and makes people seek communion. Those who are seeking this goal can allow each other a variety of religious vocabulary and still be travellers on the same path.

In a pluralistic culture without a solid centre, everyone must work on his or her own catechism, those demands which are felt as obligations. The intention of the Bible accords with this as long as it corrects people and fills them with an expectation which does not reinforce their views but disturbs them.

'Resurrection' and 'eternal life': Opening up a new sphere of life

Two important biblical terms remain for us to consider: resurrection and kingdom of God. What can they say to people of our time? What expectation does the Bible offer when it speaks of resurrection?

The first Christian community was not the immediate

result of the efforts of the earthly Jesus to give his people a better understanding of God. Rather, it came into being as a result of the appearances of Jesus after his death. These communicated to the disturbed disciples the certainty that his death had not been a wretched end but was the necessary transition to an extended, fruitful, 'eternal' activity. Short phrases like 'through the cross to the crown' or 'through death to victory' describe this experience.

In New Testament times this experience was communicated by the proclamation of 'resurrection'? Can that also be effective today? Anyone who thinks that the term resurrection has to do with the overcoming of biological death misunderstands its meaning. It is aimed at something else.

There is no life which is not bounded by death. Without it, life would not be structured by any sense of responsibility (Genesis 2.17) and thus would lack the basis for human worth. Life is a commodity in short supply: material which is not unlimitedly at our disposal. If it were not perishable, people would not value it; it would not possess its unique value. It would lose its character of decision, because we would be able to make up for what we had neglected. And in that case God, too, would have another quality. His judgment on men and women and the healing which the cross and resurrection offer to the wounded soul would then lack both their sobering and their encouraging character, i.e. their full seriousness. Peace, freedom and joy would not exist in their fullness. A life that is not endangered cannot be lost, and therefore cannot be won either. Only a premature or a violent death calls for lamentation – not biological death as such, apart from the pain of parting.

Biblical talk of resurrection seeks to show that the fruit of dying, of crucifixion – today, as for Jesus himself – is still an unknown, a new kind of life together, a growth and a liberation; a growth – comparable with that of the biblical belief when it ceased to be nationalistic, or a liberation – perhaps the readiness of enemies in our day to listen to one another and enter into dialogue despite the ongoing existence of historically conditioned differences. The biblical reports of the risen Christ do not present happenings which can be integrated into our usual experiences; rather, they provide a new framework for living. Those who want to become involved in it venture to empty themselves – as did Jesus. From antiquity baptism has been seen as the symbol for 'immersing' oneself in this new life.

'Resurrection' or the 'eternal life' that the well-to-do man in Luke 18 was to 'gain' does not mean an ongoing existence free from burdens but existence in a wider sphere in which it is possible to take risks in trust and work in freedom.

The biblical hope does not direct expectations towards an unimaginable solution of problems in an extension of life which is called the 'beyond', but points to liberation from anxiety through the cross of Jesus and the influence of the exalted Son of God on the community. People may hope that their belief in this happening will be confirmed through their experience: they can learn to follow Jesus. Learning and finding confirmation call for a constant struggle. This work on ourselves and our environment shapes our precious days; we are on the way to existing, i.e. to becoming mature. This is the content of the biblical hope.

What does this hope promise when the question of transcendence and the beyond is raised? Certainly it does not promise an existence without contradictions and tensions. That sort of existence is unimaginable and therefore cannot either strengthen us or comfort us. Rather, the believer hopes that after death, as before, he or she will go on existing and will be challenged by the prospect of success in growing. In religious language, even after death God, our loving Father, will continue to be interested in us.

Jesus was once asked by the Sadducees about the relationship between this world and the beyond (Mark 12). If a woman is married more than once, whose wife will she be in the beyond? His answer was: theoretical questions like this miss the essential features of life. Expose yourself to its challenges as your fathers did, by following the call that they encountered. Then you will experience the power of God. Or, in present-day language: then you will find that dimension opening up to you which no dispute about the relationship between this world and the beyond will ever disclose.

We should be careful that any talk of transcendence and the beyond does not distract us from the responsibility that we have for shaping the reality between birth and death that is entrusted to us. What is to hold later in a reality which we have not yet experienced is convincing only if it is true of reality now. Talk of the beyond and transcendence which arouses hopes of an easy solution to problems in a theoretical reality robs the immanent reality which we experience day by day of its unconditional importance; those who hope like this are in danger of not doing justice to this importance and evading their chance to mature. Anyone who responds to this task here has less to catch up on 'there'.

The kingdom of God: Social salvation or redemption of the soul?

In the Lord's Prayer there is a petition for the coming of the kingdom of God. What does that mean today? Social salvation or redemption of the soul?

From the time of Moses and the prophets, the biblical view of God has commended social structures of comradeship and partnership, and this recommendation is not toned down in the New Testament. But when the people of Israel was robbed of its optimistic belief in success as a result of historical catastrophes, because its obedience to God was clearly not bearing the expected political fruits, belief developed into an attitude which prevented people from drowning pitifully in the sea of disillusionment. Rather, they might be confident of being able to lead a useful, fulfilled existence after the downfall of the nation and even as a result of it. The book of Job and psalms like Psalms 23 and 73 are the classical expression of this all-embracing trust. Though body and soul may fail, God will guide us.

The Bible knows two related spheres in which life finds fulfilment: social involvement and the maturing of the character (what used to be called 'saving the soul'). The one cannot be played off against the other. God's rule in the world, his 'kingdom', does not guarantee either an ideal social structure for all the world – including those who do not believe - or a safe refuge for souls in need of rest. It is the community of *healed* souls. They see the painful consequences of human wrong-doing – in religious terms, God's judgment – not as a punishment but as God's abiding interest in them. God does not leave them to the misery in which they have imprisoned themselves, regarding them as being of no further use for his purposes. In the judgment God calls on them to respond to his call and to exist; despite their failure, he is concerned about their growth and their fulfilment. The judgment opens the door to repentance and renewal and is therefore a form of God's grace. The community of healed souls sees bearing the cross as having a positive sense and therefore can press on with full vigour towards better social structures. Its members are bound together as brothers and sisters with God as their father. They are a serving community.

This community serves in a world society the inhabitants and therefore also the structures of which tend to let the strong make themselves comfortable at the expense of the weak. So the community's service towards individuals has the aim of enabling the weak to ward off the incursions of the strong and offer resistance, and to open the eyes of the strong so that they do not just exploit the weak for themselves but also serve them. This service aims both at helping people to mature and at changing their social structures. Where this community of brothers and sisters is effective, God's kingdom is present; in so far as it works towards maturity in men and women and in social structures, it is on the way and moving towards its future consummation.

Historical developments have led to there being nowadays a number of organized religious communions which appeal to the God of the Bible: Jews, Roman Catholics, Greek Orthodox, Lutheran, Anglican, Reformed. Which is to be recommended? That is a barren question to ask; it diverts attention for the responsibility which each individual has for his or her course under God's guidance. Rather, it is helpful to ask what people can do nowadays within the churches in which they find themselves, which have been entrusted to them and which they love, to contribute to the growth there of a community of men and women who help one another to master life, with God as their common point of reference and one another as brothers and sisters.

Increased consumption as the aim of a society leads to people attempting to overtake one another. Neither a brotherly/ sisterly attitude nor partnership can flourish in such an atmosphere. Therefore there is no avoiding the question 'What aim and what social framework is necessary if we are to care for one another?' Caring for one another is a strenuous business. But only when this challenge makes its mark on everyday life do people move within the sphere of influence of the God who is concerned that they should help one another to live a fulfilled life. Otherwise God remains an alien piece of culture even for those who think that they confess him.

Nowadays we need a new attitude to work. Stress and unemployment as permanent factors in society are signs of a collective disease which also limits the scope for the biblical experience of faith. The call to react to disruptions with dignity is beyond the comprehension of people who have too much work or no work at all. Should activities which are not covered by official categories of employment, like the work of bringing up children, do-it-yourself or honorary work in serving the community not enjoy public recognition? Does paid work have to be distributed equally? Those who are overburdened with work or have no recognized work may go to church conferences and ecumenical meetings, celebrate Christmas and love church music, but they do not find here the framework in which the voice of God can gain a hearing, that voice which once called from the burning bush, stirred up Moses and led him to make his mark on history.

Those who allow themselves to be crucified turn away from themselves; they live. That this news can bring joy will remain incomprehensible to those who pray to God to grant them as quiet a life as possible. Those who find satisfaction in promoting co-operation, and are concerned that all around them shall have a life worth living, will be able to understand it.

Postscript

Those in the churches who want to express their belief in the God of the Bible to outsiders might want to put it in a creed like this:

I believe in God,
in whom we are secure.
God calls us to direct our lives
towards using all our power,
social, economic and political,
our intellect, money, sex, and art,
in the service of the one human family.

I believe in Jesus Christ.
He is given to us as the way to our fulfilment.
He accepted his failure as God's will,
and continued to be concerned
even for those who disappointed him.
The crucifixion did not hem him in and end his work,
but extended that work and made it eternal.
He became mediator between us and the unfathomable God,
and as we follow him our damaged lives are made whole.

His Spirit shapes the community of believers.
That Spirit frees us from shyness
to take responsibility for others.
We discover that our enemies are sisters and brothers,

with whom we can co-operate.
Despite obstacles and our own faults we do not become resigned,
but grow in courage, patience and knowledge.
Those who are willing to be disturbed are used;
those who repent find life.

Dates in Biblical History

(These dates are not always historically certain, and in some cases are just approximations)

c.1250 BCE	Exodus with Moses from Egypt
c.1230	Settlement of the Israelite tribes under Joshua in Canaan
	Time of the judges up to Samuel;
	Battles with the Philistine cities
1025-1005	Establishment of the kingdom by Samuel; Saul
1005-965	David, Nathan
965-926	Solomon
926	Division of Israel into north and south: Israel/Samaria and Judah/Jerusalem
c.860	Elijah in the northern kingdom
c.850	'Yahwist' in Judah
c.750	'Elohist' in Israel
760-750	Amos active in Israel
750-725	Hosea active in Israel
721	Israel conquered by Assyria (Sargon); Israel becomes the Syrian province of Samaria
746-701	Isaiah active in Jerusalem
c.700 or earlier	Zarathustra in Media/Persia
639-609	King Josiah in Jerusalem
627-585	Jeremiah active in Jerusalem
622	Discovery of 'Deuteronomy'
609	Josiah's death at Megiddo
604 (?)	Lao Tse born in China, Taoism
597 and 587	Conquest and destruction of Jerusalem by Nebuchadnezzar; end of the state of Judah; deportation of the leading classes

593-71	Ezekiel active in Babylon
566-486	Gautama Buddha in India
551-479	Confucius in China
546-538	'Second Isaiah' active in Babylon
538	Conquest of Babylon by Cyrus the Persian
537	A minority of Jews return to Jerusalem
500-460	The 'Priestly Writing' composed, largely in Babylon
From 444	Temple building by Nehemiah
From 398	Judaism consolidated as a religious community by Ezra
c.390	The books of Jonah and Ruth
323	Alexander the Great dies in Babylon
320-198	Judaea under Egyptian rule
c.300-250	Job
c.200	Ecclesiastes
c.180	Jesus Sirach
198-128	Judaea under Syrian and Hellenistic rule
175-164	Antiochus IV Epiphanes in Syria
c.170	Zechariah 9-11
167-164	The book of Daniel
From 167	The Maccabees fight for freedom
128-63	Independent Jewish state
63 BCE	Pompey in the temple; Roman rule
70 CE	Titus puts down the Jewish revolt; conquest of Jerusalem
73	Fall of Masada on the Dead Sea
135	End of Bar Kochba's revolt

Paul's dates

c.30	Crucifixion of Jesus
c.33	Christ appears to Paul before Damascus; then rather unsuccessful activity in Transjordan
35	Two weeks in Jerusalem with Peter and Paul, then in Syria (Antioch) and Cilicia/Asia Minor
48	So-called 'Apostolic Council' in Jerusalem; discussion of problems of mission among non-Jews
49	Foundation of communities in Europe: Philippi and Thessalonica
50/52	Eighteen months in Corinth (Letters to the Thessalonians)
52/55	Two and a half years in Ephesus (Galatians and I Corinthians)
55/56	In Philippi, Thessalonica (II Corinthians) and Corinth (Letter to the Romans)
Pentecost 56	Third visit to Jerusalem; arrest
56-58	In custody in Caesarea for interrogation (from there or later from Rome: Philippians and the Letter to Philemon)
Autumn 58	Transportation to Rome, shipwreck off Malta
59-61	Two years in custody in Rome for interrogation
c.70	Gospel of Mark
80-90	Gospel of Matthew and Luke-Acts
c.100	Gospel of John

Map of Palestine

References to the Bible

You will find the main references to the Bible (those between inverted commas) as indicated below. In all cases the translations are my own and sometimes they are very free.

Page 4: 'A light for the nations', Isaiah 51.4.
- 5: The second commandment, Exodus 20.2
  The calling of Moses, Exodus 3
- 14: Amos's accusations, Amos 1–2
  The day of the Lord, Amos 5.20
- 16: 'His servants the prophets', Amos 3.7
- 17: 'A remnant returns' (Shear-jashub), Isaiah 7.3
- 19: 'Lord, will you soon restore . . .', Acts 1.6
- 21: 'Cursed be the day . . .', Jeremiah 20.14
- 22: 'Everyone is punishable . . .', see Jeremiah 31.29f.
- 23: 'The soul that sins . . .', Ezekiel 18.20f.
- 25: 'Because his soul has laboured . . .', Isaiah 53.11f.
  'He was wounded for our misdeeds . . .', Isaiah 53.5f.
- 26: 'He measures the waters . . .' Isaiah 40.12
- 32: 'How shall I answer?', see Job 42.1ff.
  'God looked on him . . .', Job 42.10
- 35: 'Hear, O Israel . . .', Deuteronomy 6.4f.
- 36: 'Such a troubled time . . .', Daniel 12.1f.
- 39: 'I saw in this night vision', Daniel 7.13f.
- 40: 'Look, your king is coming . . .', Zechariah 9.9
  'Seek good and not evil', Amos 5.14
- 41: 'I saw all that is done . . .', Ecclesiastes 1.14; 3.8f.
  'Eat your bread with joy . . .', Ecclesiastes 5.18f.
- 44: 'Father, if you will, take this cup . . .', Mark 14.36.
- 45: 'You shall love the Lord your God . . .', Mark 12.29–31

46: 'Give us today our daily bread', Matthew 6.11
'Woe to you rich', Luke 6.24
'God be gracious . . .', Luke 18.13
'Anyone who looks lustfully . . .', Matthew 5.27
'Ask and it shall be given . . .', Matthew 7.7

48: 'All the things you need . . .', Matthew 6.33

49: 'Blessed are you poor . . .', Luke 6.20
'Blessed are those . . .', Matthew 5.3–10
'Are you the anointed one . . . ?', Matthew 11.2ff.

51: 'We had hoped that he would redeem Israel . . .', Luke 24.21

55: 'I am Jesus . . .', Acts 9.5
'It was reported to me . . .', I Corinthians 15.3ff.
'When it pleased God . . .', Galatians 1.15ff.

64: 'Whenever I think of you . . .', Philippians 1.3f.
'The Lord will descend . . .', I Thessalonians 4.16ff.

65: 'Do not let yourselves be deceived . . .', II Thessalonians 2.3

66: 'If anyone has come . . .', II Corinthians 5.17–21

67: 'We live in faith', II Corinthians 5.7
'Then we shall ever be with the Lord', I Thessalonians 4.16

68: 'God so loved the world . . .', John 3.16
'Anyone who hears my word . . .', John 5.24f.

75: 'If you are offering your gift . . .', Matthew 5.23